By Sir A. Quiller-Couch

On the Art of Writing

Studies in Literature

On the Art of Reading

By

Sir Arthur Quiller-Couch, M.A.

Fellow of Jesus College
King Edward VII Professor of English Literature
in the University of Cambridge

G. P. Putnam's Sons
New York and London
The Knickerbocker Press
1920

Printed in the United States of America

To

H. F. S.

AND

H. M. C.

PREFACE

THE following twelve lectures have this much in common with a previous twelve published in 1916 under the title *On the Art of Writing*—they form no compact treatise but present their central idea as I was compelled at the time to enforce it, amid the dust of skirmishing with opponents and with practical difficulties.

They cover—and to some extent, by reflection, chronicle—a period during which a few friends, who had an idea and believed in it, were fighting to establish the present English Tripos at Cambridge. In the end we carried our proposals without a vote: but the opposition was stiff for a while; and I feared, on starting to read over these pages for the press, that they might be too occasional and disputatious. I am happy to think that, on the whole, they are not; and that the reader, though he may wonder at its discursiveness, will find the argument pretty free from polemic. Any one who has inherited a library of 17th century theology will agree with me that, of all dust, the ashes of dead controversies afford the driest.

And after all, and though it be well worth while to strive that the study of English (of our own literature, and of the art of using our own language, in speech or in writing, to the best purpose) shall take an honourable place among the schools of a great university, that the other fair sisters of learning shall

> Ope for thee their queenly circle . . .

it is not in our universities that the general redemption of English will be won; nor need a mistake here or there, at Oxford or Cambridge or London, prove fatal. We make our discoveries through our mistakes: we watch one another's success: and where there is freedom to experiment there is hope to improve. A youth who can command means to enter a university can usually command some range in choosing which university it shall be. If Cambridge cannot supply what he wants, or if our standard of training be low in comparison with that of Oxford, or of London, or of Manchester, the pressure of neglect will soon recall us to our senses.

The real battle for English lies in our Elementary Schools, and in the training of our Elementary Teachers. It is there that the foundations of a sound national teaching in English will have to be laid, as it is there that a wrong trend will lead to incurable issues. For the poor child has no choice of schools, and the elementary teacher, whatever his individual gifts, will work under a yoke imposed upon him by Whitehall. I devoutly trust that Whitehall will make the yoke easy and adaptable while insisting that the chariot must be drawn.

I foresee, then, these lectures condemned as the utterances of a man who, occupying a chair, has contrived to fall betwixt two stools. My thoughts have too often strayed from my audience in a university theatre away to remote rural class-rooms where the hungry sheep look up and are not fed; to piteous groups of urchins standing at attention and chanting *The Wreck of the Hesperus* in unison. Yet to these, being tied to the place and the occasion, I have brought no real help.

A man has to perform his task as it comes. But I must say this in conclusion. Could I wipe these lectures out and re-write them in hope to benefit my countrymen in general, I should begin and end upon the text to be found in the twelfth and last—that a liberal education is not an appendage to be purchased by a few: that Humanism is, rather, a *quality* which can, and should, condition all our teaching; which can, and should, be impressed as a character upon it all, from a poor child's first lesson in reading up to a tutor's last word to his pupil on the eve of a Tripos.

ARTHUR QUILLER-COUCH.

July 7, 1920.

CONTENTS

INTRODUCTORY

I

IN the third book of the *Ethics*, and in the second chapter, Aristotle, dealing with certain actions which, though bad in themselves, admit of pity and forgiveness because they were committed involuntarily, through ignorance, instances "the man who did not know a subject was forbidden, like Æschylus with the Mysteries," and "the man who only meant to show how it worked, like the fellow who let off the catapult" (ἢ δεῖξαι βουλόμενος ἀφεῖναι, ὡς ὁ τὸν καταπέλτην).

I feel comfortably sure, Gentlemen, that in a previous course of lectures *On the Art of Writing*, unlike Æschylus, I divulged no mysteries: but I am troubled with speculations over that man and the catapult, because I really was trying to tell you how the thing worked; and Aristotle, with a reticence which (as Horace afterwards noted) may lend itself to obscurity, tells us neither what happened to that exponent of ballistics, nor to the engine itself, nor to the other person.

My discharge, such as it was, at any rate provoked another Professor (*emeritus*, learned, sagacious, venerable) to retort that the true business of a Chair such as this is to instruct young men how to *read* rather than how to write. Well, be it so. I accept the challenge.

I propose in this and some ensuing lectures, to talk of the Art and Practice of Reading, particularly as applied to English Literature: to discuss on what ground and through what faculties an Author and his Reader meet: to enquire if, or to what extent, Reading of the best Literature can be taught; and supposing it to be taught, if or to what extent it can be examined upon; with maybe an interlude or two, to beguile the way.

II

The first thing, then, to be noted about the reading of English (with which alone I am concerned) is that for Englishmen it has been made, by Act of Parliament, compulsory.

The next thing to be noted is that in our schools and colleges and universities it has been made, by statute or in practice, all but impossible.

The third step is obvious—to reconcile what we cannot do with what we must: and to that aim I shall, under your patience, direct this and the following lecture. I shall be relieved at all events, and from the outset, of the doubt by which many a Professor, here and elsewhere, has been haunted: I mean the doubt whether there really *is* such a subject as that of which he proposes to treat. Anything that requires so much human ingenuity as reading English in an English University *must* be an art.

III

But I shall be met, of course, by the question, "How is the reading of English made impossible at Cambridge?" and I pause here on the edge of my subject, to clear away that doubt.

It is no fault of the University.

The late Philip Gilbert Hamerton, whom some remember as an etcher, wrote a book which he entitled (as I think, too magniloquently) *The Intellectual Life*. He cast it in the form of letters—"To an Author who kept very Irregular Hours," "To a Young Etonian who thought of becoming a Cotton-spinner," "To a Young Gentleman who had firmly resolved never to wear anything but a Grey Coat" (but Mr. Hamerton couldn't quite have meant that). "To a Lady of High Culture who found it difficult to associate with persons of her Own Sex," "To a young Gentleman of Intellectual Tastes, who, without having as yet any particular lady in view, had expressed, in a General Way, his Determination to get Married." The volume is well worth reading. In the first letter of all, addressed "To a young Man of Letters who worked Excessively," Mr. Hamerton fishes up from his memory, for admonishment, this salutary instance:

A tradesman, whose business affords an excellent outlet for energetic bodily activity, told me that having attempted in addition to his ordinary work, to acquire a foreign language which seemed likely to be useful to him, he had been obliged to abandon it on account of alarming cerebral symptoms. This man has immense vigour and energy, but the digestive functions, in this instance, are sluggish. However, when he abandoned study, the cerebral inconveniences disappeared, and have never returned since.

IV

Now we all know, and understand, and like that man: for the simple reason that he is every one of us.

You or I (say) have to take the Modern Languages Tripos, Section A (English), in 1917.[1]   First of all (and rightly) it is demanded of us that we show an acquaintance, and something more than a bowing acquaintance, with Shakespeare.   Very well; but next we have to write a paper and answer questions on the outlines of English Literature from 1350 to 1832—almost five hundred years—, and next to write a paper and show particular knowledge of English Literature between 1700 and 1785 —eighty-five years.   Next comes a paper on passages from selected English verse and prose writings—the Statute discreetly avoids calling them literature—between 1200 and 1500, exclusive of Chaucer; with questions on language, metre, literary history and literary criticism: then a paper on Chaucer with questions on language, metre, literary history and literary criticism: lastly a paper on writing in the Wessex dialect of Old English, with questions on the cornet, flute, harp, sackbut, language, metre and literary history.

[1] This lecture was delivered October 25, 1916.   At that time I was engaged against a system of English teaching which I believed to be thoroughly bad.   That system has since given place to another, which I am prepared to defend as a better.

Now if you were to qualify yourself for all this as a scholar should, and in two years, you would certainly deserve to be addressed by Mr. Hamerton as "A Young Man of Letters who worked Excessively"; and to work excessively is not good for any one. Yet, on the other hand, you are precluded from using, for your "cerebral inconveniences," the heroic remedy exhibited by Mr. Hamerton's enterprising tradesman, since on that method you would not attain to the main object of your laudable ambition, a Cambridge degree.

But the matter is very much worse than your Statute makes it out. Take one of the papers in which some actual acquaintance with Literature is required—the Special Period from 1700 to 1785; then turn to your *Cambridge History of English Literature*, and you will find that the mere bibliography of those eighty-five years occupies something like five or six hundred pages —five or six hundred pages of titles and authors in simple enumeration! The brain reels; it already suffers "cerebral inconveniences." But stretch the list back to Chaucer, back through Chaucer to those alleged prose writings in the Wessex dialect, then forward from 1785 to Wordsworth, to Byron, to Dickens, Carlyle, Tennyson, Browning, Meredith, even to this year in which literature still lives and engenders; and the brain, if not too giddy indeed, stands as Satan stood on the brink of Chaos—

> Pondering his voyage; for no narrow frith
> He had to cross—

and sees itself, with him, now plumbing a vast vacuity, and anon nigh-foundered, "treading the crude consistence."

The whole business of reading English Literature in two years, to *know* it in any reputable sense of the word —let alone your learning to write English—is, in short, impossible. And the framers of the Statute, recognising this, have very sensibly compromised by setting you to work on such things as "the Outlines of English Literature"; which are not Literature at all but are only what some fellow has to say about it, hastily summarising his estimates of many works, of which on a generous computation he has probably read one fifth; and by examining you on (what was it all?) "language, metre, literary history and literary criticism," which again are not Literature, or at least (as a Greek would say in his idiom) escape their own notice being Literature. For English Literature as I take it, is *that which sundry men and women have written memorably in English about Life.* And so I come to my subject—the art of reading *that,* which is Literature.

V

I shall take leave to leap into it over another man's back, or, rather over two men's backs. No doubt it has happened to many of you to pick up in a happy moment some book or pamphlet or copy of verse which just says the word you have unconsciously been listening for, almost craving to speak for yourself, and so sends you

off hot-foot on the trail. And if you have had that
experience, it may also have happened to you that, after
ranging, you returned on the track "like faithful hound
returning," in gratitude, or to refresh the scent; and
that, picking up the book again, you found it no such
wonderful book after all, or that some of the magic had
faded by process of the change in yourself which itself
had originated. But the word was spoken.

Such a book—pamphlet I may call it, so small it was,
—fell into my hands some ten years ago; *The Aims of
Literary Study*—no very attractive title—by Dr. Corson, a distinguished American Professor (and let me say
that, for something more than ten—say for twenty—
years much of the most thoughtful as well as the most
thorough work upon English comes to us from America).
I find, as I handle again the small duodecimo volume,
that my own thoughts have taken me a little wide, perhaps a little astray, from its suggestions. But for
loyalty's sake I shall start just where Dr. Corson started,
with a passage from Browning's *A Death in the Desert*,
supposed (you will remember)—

Supposed of Pamphylax the Antiochene

narrating the death of St. John the Evangelist, John of
Patmos; the narrative interrupted by this gloss:

[This is the doctrine he was wont to teach,
How divers persons witness in each man,
Three souls which make up one soul: *first*, to wit,
A soul of each and all the bodily parts,

Seated therein, which works, and is *What Does*,
And has the use of earth and ends the man
Downward: but, tending upward for advice,
Grows into, and again is grown into
By the next soul, which, seated in the brain,
Useth the first with its collected use,
And feeleth, thinketh, willeth,—is *What Knows:*
Which, duly tending upward in its turn,
Grows into, and again is grown into
By the last soul, that uses both the first,
Subsisting whether they assist or no,
And, constituting man's self, is *What Is*—
And leans upon the former

(Mark the world, Gentlemen;—"*leans* upon the former"
—leaning back, as it were felt by him, on this very man
who had leaned on Christ's bosom, being loved)

And leans upon the former, makes it play,
As that played off the first: and, tending up,
Holds, is upheld by, God, and ends the man
Upward in that dread point of intercourse,
Nor needs a place, for it returns to Him.
What Does, What Knows, What Is; three souls, one man.
I give the glossa of Theotypas.]

What Does, What Knows, What Is—there is no mistaking what Browning means, nor in what degrees of hierarchy he places this, that, and the other. . . . Does it not strike you how curiously men today, with their minds perverted by hate, are inverting that order? —all the highest value set on *What Does*—*What Knows* suddenly seen to be of importance, but only as important in feeding the guns, perfecting explosives, collaring trade—all in the service of *What Does*, of "Get on or Get Out," of "Efficiency"; no one stopping to think that "Efficiency" is—must be—a relative term! Efficient for what?—for *What Does*, *What Knows* or perchance, after all, for *What Is?* No! banish the humanities and throw everybody into practical science: not into that study of natural science, which can never conflict with the "humanities" since it seeks discovery for the pure sake of truth, or charitably to alleviate man's lot—

> Sweetly, rather, to ease, loose and bind
> As need requires, this frail fallen humankind . . .

—but to invent what will be commercially serviceable in besting your neighbour, or in gassing him, or in slaughtering him neatly and wholesale. But still the whisper (not ridiculous in its day) will assert itself, that *What Is* comes first, holding and upheld by God; still through the market clamour for a "Business Government" will persist the voice of Plato murmuring that, after all, the best form of government is government by good men: and the voice of some small man faintly protesting, "But I don't want to be governed by business men; because I know them and, without asking much of life, I have a hankering to die with a shirt on my back."

VI

But let us postpone *What Is* for a moment, and deal with *What Does* and *What Knows*. They too, of course, have had their oppositions, and the very meaning of a University such as Cambridge its *fons*, its *origo*, its τό τί ἦν εἶναι—was to assert *What Knows* against *What Does* in a mediæval world pranced over by men-at-arms, Normans, English, Burgundians, Scots. Ancillary to Theology, which then had a meaning vastly different from its meaning today, the University tended as portress of the gate of knowledge—of such knowledge as the Church required, encouraged, or permitted—and kept the flag of intellectual life, as I may put it, flying above that gate and over the passing throngs of "doers" and mailed-fisters. The University was a *Seat of Learning:* the Colleges, as they sprang up, were *Houses of Learning.*

But note this, which in their origin and still in the frame of their constitution, differentiates Oxford and Cambridge from all their ancient sisters and rivals. These two (and no third, I believe, in Europe) were corporations of Teachers, existing for Teachers, governed by Teachers. In a Scottish University the students by vote choose their Rector: but here or at Oxford no undergraduate, no Bachelor, counts at all in the government, both remaining alike *in statu pupillar*, until qualified as Masters—*Magistri*. Mark the word, and mark also the title of one who obtained what in those days would be the highest of degrees (but yet gave him no voting strength above a Master). He was a Professor—"Sanctæ Theologiæ Professor." To this day every country clergyman who comes up to Cambridge to record his *non-placet*, does so by virtue of his

capacity to teach what he learned here—in theory, that
is. Scholars were included in College foundations on
a sort of pupil-teacher-supply system: living in rooms
with the lordly masters, and valeting them for the
privilege of "reading with" them. We keep to this day
the pleasant old form of words. Now for various reasons—one of which, because it is closely germane to my
subject, I shall particularly examine—Oxford and Cambridge, while conserving almost intact their mediæval
frame of government, with a hundred other survivals
which Time but makes, through endurance, more en-
dearing, have, insensibly as it were, and across (it must
be confessed) intervals of sloth and gross dereliction of
duty, added a new function to the cultivation of learning—that of furnishing out of youth a succession of
men capable of fulfilling high offices in Church and
State.

Some may regret this. I think many of us must
regret that a deeper tincture of learning is not required
of the average pass-man, or injected into him perforce.
But speaking roughly about fact, I should say that
while we elders up here are required—nay, presumed—
to *know* certain things, we aim that our young men
shall *be* of a certain kind; and I see no cause to disown a
sentence in the very first lecture I had the honour of
reading before you—"The man we are proud to send
forth from our Schools will be remarkable less for something he can take out of his wallet and exhibit for knowledge, than for *being* something, and that something
recognisable for a man of unmistakable intellectual

breeding, whose trained judgment we can trust to choose the better and reject the worse."

The reasons which have led our older universities to deflect their functions (whether for good or ill) so far from their first purpose are complicated if not many. Once admit young men in large numbers, and youth (I call any Dean or Tutor to witness) must be compromised with; will construe the laws of its seniors in its own way, now and then breaking them; and will inevitably end by getting something of its own way. The growth of gymnastic, the insensible gravitation of the elderly towards Fenner's—there to snatch a fearful joy and explain that the walk was good for them; the Union and other debating societies; College rivalries; the festivities of May Week; the invasion of women students: all these may have helped. But I must dwell discreetly on one compelling and obvious cause—the increased and increasing unwieldiness of Knowledge. And that is the main trouble, as I guess.

VII

Let us look it fair in the face: because it is the main practical difficulty with which I propose that, in succeeding lectures, we grapple. Against Knowledge I have, as the light cynic observed of a certain lady's past, only one serious objection—that there is so much of it. There is indeed so much of it that if with the best will in the world you devoted yourself to it as a mere scholar, you could not possibly digest its accumulated and still accumulating stores. As Sir Thomas Elyot wrote in the sixteenth century (using, you will observe, the very word of Mr. Hamerton's energetic but fed-up tradesman), "Inconveniences always doe happen by ingurgitation and excessive feedings." An old schoolmaster and a poet—Mr. James Rhoades, late of Sherborne— comments in words which I will quote, being unable to better them:

> This is no less true of the mind than of the body. I do not know that a well-informed man, as such, is more worthy of regard than a well-fed one. The brain, indeed, is a nobler organ than the stomach, but on that very account is the less to be excused for indulging in repletion. The temptation, I confess, is greater, because for the brain the banquet stands ever spread before our eyes, and is, unhappily, as indestructible as the widow's meal and oil.
>
> Only think what would become of us if the physical food, by which our bodies subsist, instead of being consumed by the eater, was passed on intact by every generation to the next, with the superadded hoards of all the ages, the earth's productive power meanwhile increasing year by year beneath the unflagging hand of Science, till, as Comus says, she
>
> > would be quite surcharged with her own weight
> > And strangled with her waste fertility.

Should we rather not pull down our barns, and build smaller, and make bonfires of what they would not hold? And yet, with regard to Knowledge, the very opposite of this is what we do. We store the whole religiously, and that though not twice alone, as with the bees in Virgil, but scores of times in every year, is the teeming produce gathered in. And then we put a fearful pressure on ourselves and others to gorge of it as much as ever we can hold.

Facit indignatio versus. My author, gathering heat, puts it somewhat dithyrambically: but there you have it, Gentlemen.

If you crave for Knowledge, the banquet of Knowledge grows and groans on the board until the finer appetite sickens. If, still putting all your trust in Knowledge, you try to dodge the difficulty by specialising, you produce a brain bulging out inordinately on one side, on the other cut flat down and mostly paralytic at that: and in short so long as I hold that the Creator has an idea of a man, so long shall I be sure that no uneven specialist realises it. The real tragedy of the Library at Alexandria was not that the incendiaries burned immensely, but that they had neither the leisure nor the taste to discriminate.

VIII

The old schoolmaster whom I quoted just now goes on:

I believe, if the truth were known, men would be astonished at the small amount of learning with which a high degree of culture is compatible. In a moment of enthusiasm I ventured once to tell my "English set" that if they could really master the ninth book of *Paradise Lost*, so as to rise to the height of its great argument and incorporate all its beauties in themselves, they would at one blow, by virtue of that alone, become highly cultivated men. . . . More and more various learning might raise them to the same height by different paths, but could hardly raise them higher.

Here let me interpose and quote the last three lines of that Book—three lines only; simple, unornamented, but

for all men and women who have dwelt together
since our first parents, in mere statement how wise!

> Thus they in mutual accusation spent
> The fruitless hours, *but neither self-condemning;*
> And of their vain contest appear'd no end.

A parent afterwards told me (my schoolmaster adds) that
his son went home and so buried himself in the book that
food and sleep that day had no attraction for him. Next
morning, I need hardly say, the difference in his appearance
was remarkable: he had outgrown all his intellectual clothes.

The end of this story strikes me, I confess, as vapid,
and may be compared with that of the growth of
Delian Apollo in the Homeric hymn; but we may
agree that, in reading, it is not quantity so much that
tells, as quality and thoroughness of digestion.

IX

What Does—What Knows—What Is. . . .

I am not likely to depreciate to you the value of *What
Does*, after spending my first twelve lectures up here, on
the art and practice of Writing, encouraging you to *do*
this thing which I daily delight in trying to do: as God
forbid that any one should hint a slightening word of
what our sons and brothers are doing just now, and
doing for us! But Peace being the normal condition of
man's activity, I look around me for a vindication of
what is noblest in *What Does* and am content with a
passage from George Eliot's poem *Stradivarius*, the gist

of which is that God himself might conceivably make
better fiddles than Stradivari's, but by no means certainly; since, as a fact, God orders his best fiddles of
Stradivari. Says the great workman,

                              "God be praised,
Antonio Stradivari has an eye
That winces at false work and loves the true,
With hand and arm that play upon the tool
As willingly as any singing bird
Sets him to sing his morning roundelay,
Because he likes to sing and likes the song."
Then Naldo: "'Tis a pretty kind of fame
At best, that comes of making violins;
And saves no masses, either.   Thou wilt go
To purgatory none the less."
                              But he:
"'Twere purgatory here to make them ill;
And for my fame—when any master holds
'Twixt chin and hand a violin of mine,
He will be glad that Stradivari lived,
Made violins, and made them of the best.
The masters only know whose work is good:
They will choose mine, and while God gives them skill
I give them instruments to play upon,
God choosing me to help Him."
                              "What! Were God
At fault for violins, thou absent?"
                                    "Yes;
He were at fault for Stradivari's work."
"Why, many hold Guiseppe's violins
As good as thine."
                        "May be: they are different.
His quality declines: he spoils his hand
With over-drinking.   But were his the best,
He could not work for two.   My work is mine.
And heresy or not, if my hand slacked

I should rob God—since He is fullest good—
Leaving a blank instead of violins.
I say, not God Himself can make man's best
Without best men to help him. . . .
                                        'Tis God gives skill,
But not without men's hands: He could not make
Antonio Stradivari's violins
Without Antonio.   Get thee to thy easel."

So much then for *What Does;* I do not depreciate it.

X

Neither do I depreciate—in Cambridge, save the mark!—*What Knows.* All knowledge is venerable; and I suppose you will find the last vindication of the scholar's life at its baldest in Browning's *A Grammarian's Funeral:*

Others mistrust and say, "But time escapes:
            Live now or never!"
He said, "What's time?   Leave Now for dog and apes!
            Man has Forever."
Back to his book then; deeper drooped his head:
            Calculus racked him:
Leaden before, his eyes grew dross of lead:
            Tussis attacked him . . .
So, with the throttling hands of death at strife,
            Ground he at grammar;
Still, thro' the rattle, parts of speech were rife:
            While he could stammer
He settled *Hoti's* business—let it be!—
            Properly based *Oun*—
Gave us the doctrine of the enclitic *De,*
            Dead from the waist down.

Well, here's the platform, here's the proper place:
  Hail to your purlieus,
All ye highfliers of the feathered race,
  Swallows and curlews!
Here's the top-peak; the multitude below
  Live, for they can, there:
This man decided not to Live but Know—
  Bury this man there.

Nevertheless Knowledge is not, cannot be, everything; and indeed, as a matter of experience, cannot even be counted upon to educate. Some of us have known men of extreme learning who yet are, some of them, uncouth in conduct, others violent and overbearing in converse, others unfair in controversy, others even unscrupulous in action—men of whom the sophist Thrasymachus in Plato's *Republic* may stand for the general type. Nay, some of us will subscribe with the old schoolmaster whom I will quote again, when he writes:

To myself personally, as an exception to the rule that opposites attract, a very well-informed person is an object of terror. His mind seems to be so full of facts that you cannot, as it were, see the wood for the trees; there is no room for perspective, no lawns and glades for pleasure and repose, no vistas through which to view some towering hill or elevated temple; everything in that crowded space seems of the same value: he speaks with no more awe of *King Lear* than of the last Cobden prize essay; he has swallowed them both with the same ease, and got the facts safe in his pouch; but he has no time to ruminate because he must still be swallowing; nor does he seem to know what even Macbeth, with Banquo's murderers then at work, found leisure to remember—that good digestion must wait on appetite, if health is to follow both.

Now that may be put a trifle too vivaciously, but the moral is true. Bacon tells us that reading maketh a full man. Yes, and too much of it makes him too full. The two words of the Greek upon knowledge remain true, that the last triumph of Knowledge is *Know Thyself*. So Don Quixote repeats it to Sancho Panza, counselling him how to govern his Island:

First, O son, thou hast to fear God, for in fearing Him is wisdom, and being wise thou canst not err.

But secondly thou hast to set thine eyes on what thou art, endeavouring to *know thyself—which is the most difficult knowledge that can be conceived.*

But to know oneself is to know that which alone can know *What Is.* So the hierarchy runs up.

XI

What Does, What Knows, What Is. . . .

I have happily left myself no time to-day to speak of *What Is:* happily, because I would not have you even approach it towards the end of an hour when your attention must be languishing. But I leave you with two promises, and with two sayings from which as this lecture took its start its successors will proceed.

The first promise is, that *What Is*, being the spiritual element in man, is the highest object of his study.

The second promise is that, nine tenths of what is

worthy to be called Literature being concerned with this spiritual element, for that it should be studied, from firstly up to ninthly, before anything else.

And my two quotations are for you to ponder:

(1) This, first:

That all spirit is mutually attractive, as all matter is mutually attractive, is an ultimate fact beyond which we cannot go. . . . Spirit to spirit—as in water face answereth to face, so the heart of man to man.

(2) And this other, from the writings of an obscure Welsh clergyman of the seventeenth century:

You will never enjoy the world aright till the sea itself floweth in your veins, till you are clothed with the heavens and crowned with the stars.

APPREHENSION *VERSUS* COMPREHENSION

I

LET us attempt to-day, Gentlemen, picking up the scent where we left at the conclusion of my first lecture, to hunt the Art of Reading (as I shall call it), a little further on the line of common-sense; then to cast back and chase on a line somewhat more philosophical. If these lines run wide and refuse to unite, we shall have made a false cast: if they converge and meet, we shall have caught our hare and may proceed, in subsequent lectures, to cook him.

Well, the line of common-sense has brought us to this point—that, man and this planet being such as they are, for a man to read all the books existent on it is impossible; and, if possible, would be in the highest degree undesirable. Let us, for example, go back quite beyond the invention of printing and try to imagine a man who had read all the rolls destroyed in the Library of Alexandria by successive burnings. (Some reckon the number of these MSS. at 700,000.) Suppose, further, this man to be gifted with a memory retentive as Lord Macaulay's. Suppose lastly that we go to such a man and beg him to repeat to us some chosen one of the fifty or seventy lost, or partially lost, plays of Euripides. It is incredible that he could gratify us.

There was, as I have said, a great burning at Alexandria in 47 B.C., when Cæsar set the fleet in the harbour on fire to prevent its falling into the hands of the Egyptians. The flames spread, and the great library stood but 400 yards from the quayside, with warehouses full of books yet closer. The last great burning was perpetrated in A.D. 642. Gibbon quotes the famous sentence of Omar, the great Mohammedan who gave the order: "If these writings of the Greeks agree with the book of God, they are useless and need not be preserved; if they disagree, they are pernicious and ought to be destroyed," and goes on:

The sentence was executed with blind obedience; the volumes of paper or parchment were distributed to the four thousand baths of the city; and such was their incredible multitude that six months were barely sufficient for the consumption of this precious fuel. . . . The tale has been repeatedly transcribed; and every scholar, with pious indignation, has deplored the irreparable shipwreck of the learning, the arts, and the genius, of antiquity. *For my own part, I am strongly tempted to deny both the fact and the consequences.*

Of the consequence he writes:

Perhaps the church and seat of the patriarchs might be enriched with a repository of books: but, if the ponderous mass of Arian and Monophysite controversy were indeed consumed in the public baths, a philosopher may allow, with a smile, that it was ultimately devoted to the benefit of mankind. I sincerely regret the more valuable libraries which have been involved in the ruin of the Roman empire; but, when I seriously compute the lapse of ages, the waste of ignorance, and the calamities of war, our treasures, rather than our losses, are the object of my surprise. Many curious and interesting facts are buried in oblivion: the three great historians of Rome have been transmitted to our hands in a mutilated state, and we are deprived of many pleasing compositions of the lyric, iambic, and dramatic poetry of the Greeks. Yet we should gratefully remember that the mischances of time and accident have spared the classic works to which the suffrage of antiquity had adjudged the first place of genius and glory; the teachers of ancient knowledge, who are still extant, had perused and compared the writings of their predecessors; nor can it fairly be presumed that any important truth, any useful discovery in art or nature, has been snatched away from the curiosity of modern ages.

I certainly do not ask you to subscribe to all that. In fact when Gibbon asks us to remember gratefully "that the mischances of time and accident have spared the classic works to which the suffrage of antiquity has adjudged the first place of genius and glory," I submit with all respect that he talks nonsense. Like the stranger in the temple of the sea-god, invited to admire the many votive garments of those preserved out of shipwreck, I ask "at ubi sunt vestimenta eorum qui post vota nuncupata perierunt?"—or in other words "Where are the trousers of the drowned?" "What about the *Sthenoboea* of Euripides, the *Revellers* of Ameipsias— to which, as a matter of simple fact, what you call the suffrage of antiquity *did* adjudge the first prize, above Aristophanes's best?"

But of course he is equally right to this extent, that

the fire consumed a vast deal of rubbish: solid tons more than any man could swallow,—let be, digest—"read, mark, learn and inwardly digest." And that was in 642 A.D., whereas we have arrived at 1916. Where would our voracious Alexandrian be to-day, with all the literature of the Middle Ages added to his feast and on top of that all the printed books of 450 years? "Reading" says Bacon, "maketh a Full Man." Yes, indeed!

Now I am glad that sentence of Bacon falls pat here, because it gives me, turning to his famous Essay *Of Studies* the reinforcement of his great name for the very argument which I am directing against the fallacy of those teachers who would have you use "manuals" as anything else than guides to your own reading, or as perspective in which the authors are set out in the respective eminence by which they claim priority of study or indicate the proportions of a literary period. Some of these manuals are written by men of knowledge so encyclopædic that (if it go with critical judgment) for these purposes they may be trusted. But to require *you*, at your stage of reading, to have even the minor names by heart is a perversity of folly. For later studies it seems to me a more pardonable mistake, but yet a mistake, to hope that by the employ of separate specialists you can get even in fifteen or twenty volumes a perspective, a proportionate description, of what English Literature really *is*. But worst of all is that Examiner, who—aware that you must please him, to get a good degree, and being just as straight and industrious as any one else—assumes that in two years you have become expert in knowledge that beats a lifetime, and, brought up against the practical impossibility of this assumption, questions you—not on a little selected first-hand knowledge—but on massed information which at the best can be but derivative and second-hand.

Now hear Bacon.

Studies serve for Delight——

(Mark it,—he puts delight first.)

Studies serve for Delight, for Ornament, and for Ability. Their Chiefe use for Delight, is in Privatenesse and Retiring;[1] for Ornament, is in Discourse; and for Ability, is in the Judgement and Disposition of Businesse. . . .   To spend too much Time in Studies is Sloth; to use them too much for Ornament is Affectation; to make Judgement wholly by their Rules is the Humour of a Scholler.   They perfect Nature, and are perfected by Experience: for Naturall Abilities are like Naturall Plants, they need Proyning by Study.   And Studies themselves doe give forth Directions too much at Large, unless they be bounded in by experience.

Again, he says:

Some Bookes are to be Tasted, Others to be Swallowed, and Some Few to be Chewed and Digested: that is, some Bookes are to be read onely in Parts; Others to be read but

---

[1] Do you remember, by the bye, Samuel Rogers's lines on Lady Jane Grey? They have always seemed to me very beautiful:

Like her most gentle, most unfortunate,
Crown'd but to die—who in her chamber sate
Musing with Plato, though the horn was blown,
And every ear and every heart was won,
And all in green array were chasing down the sun!

not Curiously; and some Few are to be read wholly, and
with Diligence and Attention. Some Bookes also may be
read by Deputy, and Extracts made of them by Others.
But that would be onely in the lesse important Arguments,
and the Meaner Sort of Bookes: else distilled Bookes are
like Common distilled Waters, Flashy Things.

So you see, Gentlemen, while pleading before you
that Reading is an Art—that its best purpose is not to
accumulate Knowledge but to produce, to educate, such-
and-such a man—that 'tis a folly to bite off more than
you can assimilate—and that with it, as with every other
art, the difficulty and the discipline lie in selecting out
of vast material, what is fit, fine, applicable—I have
the great Francis Bacon himself towering behind my
shoulder for patron.

Some would push the argument further than—here
and now, at any rate—I choose to do, or perhaps would
at all care to do. For example, Philip Gilbert Hamerton, whom I quoted to you three weeks ago, instances
in his book *The Intellectual Life* an accomplished French
cook who, in discussing his art, comprised the whole
secret of it under two heads—the knowledge of the
mutual influences of ingredients, and the judicious
management of heat:

Amongst the dishes for which my friend had a deserved
reputation was a certain *gâteau de foie* which had a very
exquisite flavour. The principal ingredient, not in quantity
but in power, was the liver of a fowl; but there were several
other ingredients also, and amongst these a leaf or two of
parsley. He told me that the influence of the parsley was a
good illustration of his theory about his art. If the parsley

were omitted, the flavour he aimed at was not produced at
all; but, on the other hand, if the quantity of the parsley
was in the least excessive, then the *gâteau* instead of being a
delicacy for *gourmets* became an uneatable mess. Perceiv-
ing that I was really interested in the subject, he kindly
promised a practical evidence of his doctrine, and the next
day intentionally spoiled the dish by a trifling addition of
parsley. He had not exaggerated the consequences; the
delicate flavour entirely departed, and left a nauseous bitter-
ness in its place, like the remembrance of an ill-spent youth.

I trust that none of you are in a position to appreciate
the full force of this last simile; and, for myself, I should
have taken the *chef's* word for it, without experiment.
Mr. Hamerton proceeds to draw his moral:

There is a sort of intellectual chemistry which is quite as
marvellous as material chemistry and a thousand times more
difficult to observe. One general truth may, however, be
relied upon. . . . It is true that *everything* we learn affects
the *whole* character of the mind.

Consider how incalculably important becomes the question of *proportion* in our knowledge, and how that which we
are is dependent as much upon our ignorance as our science.
What we call ignorance is only a smaller proportion—what
we call science only a larger.

Here the argument begins to become delicious:

The larger quantity is recommended as an unquestionable
good, but the goodness of it is entirely dependent *on the
mental product that we want*. Aristocracies have always instinctively felt this, and have decided that a gentleman
ought not to know too much of certain arts and sciences.
The character which they had accepted as their ideal would
have been destroyed by indiscriminate additions to those

ingredients of which long experience had fixed the exact proportions. . . .

The last generation of the English country aristocracy was particularly rich in characters whose unity and charm was dependent upon the limitations of their culture, and which would have been entirely altered, perhaps not for the better, by simply knowing a science or a literature that was closed to them.

If anything could be funnier than that, it is that it is, very possibly, true. Let us end our quest-by-common-sense, for the moment, on this; that to read all the books that have been written—in short to keep pace with those that are being written—is starkly impossible, and (as Aristotle would say) about what is impossible one does not argue. We *must* select. Selection implies skilful practice. Skilful practice is only another term for Art. So far plain common-sense leads us. On this point, then, let us set up a rest and hark back.

II

Let us cast back to the three terms of my first lecture —*What Does, What knows, What is.*

I shall here take leave to recapitulate a brief argument much sneered at a few years ago when it was still fashionable to consider Hegel a greater philosopher than Plato. Abbreviating it I repeat it, because I believe in it yet to-day, when Hegel (for causes unconnected with pure right and wrong) has gone somewhat out of fashion for a while.

As the tale, then, is told by Plato, in the tenth book

of *The Republic*, one Er the son of Arminius, a Pam-
phylian, was slain in battle; and ten days afterwards,
when they collected the dead for burial, his body alone
showed no taint of corruption.   His relatives, however,
bore it off to the funeral pyre; and on the twelfth day,
lying there, he returned to life, and he told them what
he had seen in the other world.   Many wonders he related concerning the dead, for example, with their
rewards and punishments: but what had impressed him
as most wonderful of all was the great spindle of Necessity, reaching up to Heaven, with the planets revolving
around it in graduated whorls of width and spread: yet
all concentric and so timed that all complete the full
circle punctually together—"The Spindle turns on the
knees of Necessity; and on the rim of each whorl sits
perched a Siren who goes round with it, hymning a
single note; the eight notes together forming one
harmony."

Now as—we have the divine word for it—upon two
great commandments hang all the law and the prophets,
so all religions, all philosophies, hang upon two stead-
fast and faithful beliefs; the first of which Plato would
show by the above parable.

It is, of course, that the stability of the Universe rests
upon ordered motion—that the "firmament" above,
around, beneath, stands firm, continues firm, on a
balance of active and tremendous forces somehow har-
moniously composed. Theology asks "by What?" or
"by Whom?" Philosophy inclines rather to ask "How?"
Natural Science, allowing that for the present these

questions are probably unanswerable, contents itself
with mapping and measuring what it can of the various
forces.   But all agree about the harmony; and when a
Galileo or a Newton discovers a single rule of it for us,
he but makes our assurance surer.   For uncounted centuries before ever hearing of Gravitation men knew of
the sun that he rose and set, of the moon that she waxed
and waned, of the tides that they flowed and ebbed, all
regularly, at times to be predicted; of the stars that
they swung as by clockwork around the pole.   Says
the son of Sirach:

> At the word of the Holy One they will stand in due order,
> And they will not faint in their watches.

So evident is this calculated harmony that men, seeking
to interpret it by what was most harmonious in themselves or in their human experience, supposed an actual
Music of the Spheres inaudible to mortals: Plato as
we see (who learned of Pythagoras) inventing his Oc-
tave of Sirens, perched on the whorls of the great
spindle and intoning as they spin.

Dante (Chaucer copying him in *The Parlement of
Foules*) makes the spheres nine: and so does Milton:

> then listen I
> To the celestial *Sirens* harmony,
> That sit upon the nine infolded Sphears,
> And sing to those that hold the vital shears,
> And turn the Adamantine spindle round
> On which the fate of gods and men is wound.
> Such sweet compulsion doth in musick lie
> To lull the daughters of *Necessity*,

And keep unsteady Nature to her law,
And the low world in measur'd motion draw
After the heavenly tune. . . .

If the sceptical mind object to the word *law* as begging the question and postulating a governing intelligence with a governing will—if it tell me that when revolted Lucifer uprose in starlight—

> and at the stars,
> Which are the brain of heaven, he look'd, and sank.
> Around the ancient track march'd, rank on rank,
> The army of unalterable law—

he was merely witnessing a series of predicable or invariable recurrences, I answer that he may be right, it suffices for my argument that they *are* recurrent, are invariable, can be predicted. Anyhow the Universe is not Chaos (if it were, by the way, we should be unable to reason about it at all). It stands and is renewed upon a harmony: and what Plato called "Necessity" is the Duty—compulsory or free as you or I can conceive it—the Duty of all created things to obey that harmony, the Duty of which Wordsworth tells in his noble Ode.

Thou dost preserve the stars from wrong:
And the most ancient heavens, through Thee, are fresh
    and strong.

III

Now the other and second great belief is, that the Universe, the macrocosm, cannot be apprehended at all except as its rays converge upon the eye, brain, soul of Man, the microcosm: on you, on me, on the tiny percipient centre upon which the immense cosmic circle focusses itself as the sun upon a burning-glass—and he is not shrivelled up! Other creatures, he notes, share in his sensations; but, so far as he can discover, not in his percipience—or not in any degree worth measuring. So far as he can discover, he is not only a bewildered actor in the great pageant but "the ring enclosing all," the sole intelligent spectator. Wonder of wonders, it is all meant for *him!*

I doubt if, among men of our nation, this truth was ever more clearly grasped than by the Cambridge Platonists who taught your forerunners of the seventeenth century. But I will quote you here two short passages from the work of a sort of poor relation of theirs, a humble Welsh parson of that time, Thomas Traherne—unknown until the day before yesterday— from whom I gave you one sentence in my first lecture. He is speaking of the fields and streets that were the scene of his childhood:

Those pure and virgin apprehensions I had from the womb, and that divine light wherewith I was born, are the best unto this day wherein I can see the Universe. . . . The corn was orient and immortal wheat, which never should be reaped, nor was ever sown. I thought it had stood from everlasting to everlasting. The dust and stones of the street were as precious as gold: the gates were at first the end of the world. The green trees, when I saw them first through one of the gates transported and ravished me. . . . Boys and girls tumbling in the street and playing

were moving jewels; I knew not that they were born or
should die. . . .

The streets were mine, the temple was mine, the people
were mine, their clothes and gold and silver were mine, as
much as their sparkling eyes, fair skins, and ruddy faces.
The skies were mine, and so were the sun, and moon, and
stars; and all the World was mine, and I the only spectator
and enjoyer of it.

Then:

> News from a foreign country came,
>   As if my treasure and my wealth lay there;
> So much it did my heart inflame,
>   'Twas wont to call my Soul into mine ear;
>   Which thither went to meet
>   The approaching sweet,
>   And on the threshold stood
>   To entertain the unknown Good. . . .
>
> What sacred instinct did inspire
> My Soul in childhood with a hope so strong?
>   What secret force moved my desire
> To expect new joys beyond the seas, so young?
>   Felicity I knew
>   Was out of view,
>
> And being here alone,
>   I saw that happiness was gone
> From me! *For* this
>   I thirsted absent bliss,
> And thought that sure beyond the seas,
>   Or else in something near at hand—
> I knew not yet (since naught did please
>   I knew) my Bliss did stand.
>
> But little did the infant dream
>   That all the treasures of the world were by:

3

And that himself was so the cream
And crown of all which round about did lie.
   Yet thus it was: the Gem,
     The Diadem,
   The Ring enclosing all
     That stood upon this earthly ball,
   The Heavenly Eye,
     Much wider than the sky,
   Wherein they all included were,
     The glorious Soul, that was the King
   Made to possess them did appear
     A small and little thing!

And then comes the noble sentence of which I promised you that it should fall into its place:

You never enjoy the world aright till the sea itself floweth in your veins, till you are clothed with the heavens and crowned with the stars.

Man in short—you, I, any one of us—the heir of it all!
Tot circa unum caput tumultuantes deos!
Our best privilege to sing our short lives out in tune with the heavenly concert—and if to sing afterwards, then afterwards!

IV

But how shall Man ever attain to understand and find his proper place in this Universe, this great sweeping harmonious circle of which nevertheless he feels himself to be the diminutive focus. His senses are absurdly imperfect. His ear cannot catch any music the spheres make; and moreover there are probably neither spheres nor music. His eye is so dull an instrument that (as

Blanco White's famous sonnet reminds us) he can neither see this world in the dark, nor glimpse any of the scores of others until it falls dark:

If Light can thus deceive, wherefore not Life?

Yet the Universal Harmony is meaningless and nothing to man save in so far as *he* apprehends it: and lacking him (so far as he knows) it utterly lacks the compliment of an audience.   Is all the great orchestra designed for nothing but to please its Conductor?   Yes, if you choose: but no, as I think.   And here my other quotation:

That all spirit is mutually attractive, as all matter is mutually attractive, is an ultimate fact. . . .   Spirit to spirit—as in water face answereth to face, so the heart of man to man.

Yes, and, all spirit being mutually attractive, far more than this!   I preach to you that, through help of eyes that are dim, of ears that are dull, by instinct of something yet undefined—call it soul—it wants no less a name—Man has a native impulse and attraction and yearning to merge himself in that harmony and be one with it: a spirit of adoption (as St. Paul says) whereby we cry *Abba, Father!*

And because ye are Sons, God hath sent forth the Spirit of His Son into your hearts, crying *Abba, Father*.

That is to say, we know we have something within us correspondent to the harmony, and (I make bold to say)

unless we have deadened it with low desires, worthy to
join in it. Even in his common daily life Man is for
ever seeking after harmony, in avoidance of chaos: he
cultivates habits by the clock, he forms committees,
governments, hierarchies, laws, constitutions, by which
(as he hopes) a system of society will work in tune. But
these are childish imitations, underplay on the great
motive:

The Kingdom of God is within you.
Quid aliud est anima quam Deus in corpore humano
    hospitans?

V

Gentlemen, you may be thinking that I have brought
you a long way round, that the hour is wearing late, and
that we are yet far from the prey we first hunted on the
line of common-sense. But be patient for a minute or
two, for almost we have our hand on the animal.

If the Kingdom of God, or anything correspondent
to it, be within us, even in such specks of dust as we
separately are, why that, and that only, can be the light
by which you or I may hope to read the universal: that
and that only, deserves the name of "*What Is.*" Nay,
I can convince you in a moment. Let me recall a passage of Emerson quoted by me on the morning I first had
the honour to address an audience in Cambridge:

It is remarkable (says he) that involuntarily we always
read as superior beings. Universal history, the poets, the
romancers, do not in their stateliest pictures . . . anywhere

make us feel that we intrude, that this is for better men;
but rather is it true that in their grandest strokes we feel
most at home. All that Shakespeare says of the king,
yonder slip of a boy that reads in the corner feels to be true
of himself.

It is remarkable, as Emerson says; and yet, as we
now see, quite simple. A learned man may patronize
a less learned one: but the Kingdom of God cannot
patronize the Kingdom of God, the larger the smaller.
There *are* large and small. Between these two mysteries
of a harmonious universe and the inward soul are
granted to live among us certain men whose minds and
souls throw out filaments more delicate than ours,
vibrating to far messages which they bring home, to
report them to us; and these men we call prophets,
poets, masters, great artists, and when they write it, we
call their report literature. But it is by the spark in us
that we read it; and not all the fire of God that was in
Shakespeare can dare to patronize the little spark in
me. If it did, I can see—with Blake—the angelic host

> throw down their spears
> And water heaven with their tears.

VI

To nurse that spark, common to the king, the sage,
the poorest child—to fan, to draw up to a flame, to
"educate" *What Is*—to recognize that it is divine, yet
frail, tender, sometimes easily tired, easily quenched
under piles of book-learning—to let it run at play very

often, even more often to let it rest in what Wordsworth
calls

<blockquote>a wise passiveness</blockquote>

passive—to use a simile of Coventry Patmore—as a
photographic plate which finds stars that no telescope
can discover, simply by waiting with its face turned
upward—to mother it, in short, as wise mothers do
their children—this is what I mean by the Art of
Reading.

For all great Literature, I would lastly observe, is
gentle towards that spirit which learns of it. It teaches
by *apprehension*, not by *comprehension*—which is what
many philosophers try to do, and, in trying, break their
jugs and spill the contents. Literature understands man
and of what he is capable. Philosophy, on the other
hand, may not be "harsh and crabbed, as dull fools suppose," but the trouble with most of its practitioners is
that they try to *comprehend* the universe. Now the
man who could comprehend the universe would *ipso
facto* comprehend God, and be *ipso facto* a Super-God,
able to dethrone him, and in the arrogance of his intellectual conceit full ready to make the attempt.

CHILDREN'S READING (I)

I HAVE often wished, Gentlemen, that some more winning name could be found for the thing we call Education; and I have sometimes thought wistfully that, had we made a better thing of it, we should long ago have found a more amiable, a blither, name.

For after all it concerns the child; and is it quite an accident that, weaning him away from lovely things that so lovelily call themselves "love," "home," "mother," we can find no more alluring titles for the streets into which we entrap him than "Educational Facilities," "Local Examinations," "Preceptors," "Pedagogues," "Professors," "Matriculations," "Certificates," "Diplomas," "Seminaries," "Elementary or Primary, and Secondary Codes," "Continuation Classes," "Reformatories," "Inspectors," "Local Authorities," "Provided" and "Non-Provided," "Denominational" and "Undenominational," and "D.-Litt." and "Mus. Bac."? Expressive terms, no doubt! —but I ask with the poet

> Who can track
> A Grace's naked foot amid them all?

Take even such words as should be perennially beautiful by connotation—words such as "Academy," "Mu-

seum." Does the one (O, *Ode* on a Distant Prospect of
Clapham Academy!) call up visions of that green lawn
by Cephissus, of its olives and plane trees and the
mirrored statues among which Plato walked and held
discourse with his few? Does the other as a rule
invite to haunts (O God! O Montreal!) where you can
be secure of communion with Apollo and the Nine?
Answer if the word Academy does not first call up to
the mind some place where small boys are crammed, the
word Museum some place where bigger game are stuffed?

And yet "academy," "museum," even "education"
are sound words if only we would make the things
correspond with their meanings. The meaning of
"education" is a leading out, a drawing-forth; not an
imposition of something on somebody—a catechism or
an uncle—upon the child; but an eliciting of what is
within him. Now, if you followed my last lecture, we
find that which is within him to be no less, potentially,
than the Kingdom of God.

I grant that this potentiality is, between the ages of
four and sixteen, not always, perhaps not often, evident.
The boy—in Bagehot's phrase "the small apple-eating
urchin whom we know"—has this in common with the
fruit for which he congenitally sins, that his very virtues
in immaturity are apt, setting the teeth on edge, to be
mistaken for vices. A writer, to whom I shall recur,
has said:

If an Englishman who had never before tasted an apple
were to eat one in July, he would probably come to the conclusion that it was a hard, sour, indigestible fruit, "con-

ceived in sin and shapen in iniquity," fit only to be consigned to perdition (on a dust heap or elsewhere). But if the same man were to wait till October and then eat an apple from the same tree, he would find that the sourness had ripened into wholesome and refreshing acidity; the hardness into firmness of fibre which, besides being pleasant to the palate, makes the apple "keep" better than any other fruit; the indigestibility into certain valuable dietetic qualities, and so on. . . .

In other words—trench, manure, hoe, and water around your young tree, and patiently allow the young fruit to develop of its own juice from the root; your own task being, as the fruit forms, but to bring in all you can of air and sunshine upon it. It must, as every mother and nurse knows, be coaxed to realize itself, to develop, to grow from its individual root. It may be coaxed and trained. But the main secret lies in encouraging it to grow, and, to that end, in pouring sunshine upon it and hoeing after each visitation of tears parentally induced.

Every child wants to grow. Every child wants to learn. During his first year or so of life he fights for bodily nutriment, almost ferociously. From the age of two or thereabouts he valiantly essays the conquest of articulate speech, using it first to identify his father or his mother amid the common herd of Gentiles; next, to demand a more liberal and varied dietary; anon, as handmaid of his imperious will to learn. This desire, still in the nursery, climbs—like dissolution in Wordsworth's sonnet—from low to high: from a craving to discover experimentally what the stomach will assimilate and what reject up to a kingly debonair interest in teleology. Our young gentleman is perfectly at ease in Sion. He wants to know why soldiers are (or were) red, and if they were born so; whence bread and milk is derived, and would it be good manners to thank the next cow for both; why mamma married papa, and— that having been explained and thoughtfully accepted as the best possible arrangement—still thoughtfully, not in the least censoriously, "why the All-Father has not married yet?" He falls asleep weighing the eligibility of various spinsters, church-workers, in the parish.

His brain teeming with questions he asks them of impulse and makes his discoveries with joy. He passes to a school, which is supposed to exist for the purpose of answering these or cognate questions even before he asks them: and behold, he is not happy! Or, he is happy enough at play, or at doing in class the things that should not be done in class: his master writes home that he suffers in his school work "from having always more animal spirits than are required for his immediate purposes." What is the trouble? You cannot explain it by home-sickness: for it attacks day boys alike with boarders. You cannot explain it by saying that all true learning involves "drudgery," unless you make that miserable word a mendicant and force it to beg the question. "Drudgery" is *what you feel to be drudgery*—

> Who sweeps a room, as for thy laws,
> Makes that and th' action fine.

—and, anyhow, this child learned one language— English, a most difficult one—eagerly. Of the nursery through which I passed only one sister wept while learning to read, and that was over a scholastic work entitled *Reading Without Tears*.

Do you know a chapter in Mr. William Canton's book *The Invisible Playmate* in which, as Carlyle dealt in *Sartor Resartus* with an imaginary treatise by an imaginary Herr Teufelsdröckh, as Matthew Arnold in *Friendship's Garland* with the imaginary letters of an imaginary Arminius (Germany in long-past happier days lent the world these playful philosophical spirits) so the later author invents an old village grandpapa, with the grandpapa-name of Altegans and a prose-poem printed in scarecrow duodecimo on paper-bag pages and entitled *"Erster Schulgang,"* "first school-going," or "first day at school"?

The poem opens with a wonderful vision of children; delightful as it is unexpected; as romantic in presentment as it is commonplace in fact. All over the world—and all under it too, when their time comes—the children are trooping to school. The great globe swings round out of the dark into the sun; there is always morning somewhere; and for ever in this shifting region of the morning-light the good Altegans sees the little ones afoot—shining companies and groups, couples and bright solitary figures; for they all seem to have a soft heavenly light about them.

He sees them in country lanes and rustic villages; on lonely moorlands . . . he sees them on the hillsides . . . in the woods, on the stepping-stones that cross the brook in the glen, along the sea-cliffs and on the water-ribbed sands; trespassing on the railway lines, making short cuts

through the corn, sitting in the ferry-boats; he sees them in
the crowded streets of smoky cities, in small rocky islands,
in places far inland where the sea is known only as a strange
tradition.

The morning-side of the planet is alive with them: one
hears their pattering footsteps everywhere. And as the vast
continents sweep "eastering out of the high shadow which
reaches beyond the moon" . . . and as new nations with
their cities and villages, their fields, woods, mountains, and
sea-shores, rise up into the morning-side, lo! fresh troops,
and still fresh troops, and yet again fresh troops of these
school-going children of the dawn.

What are weather and season to this incessant panorama
of childhood? The pigmy people trudge through the snow
on moor and hill-side; wade down flooded roads; are not to
be daunted by wind or rain, frost or the white smother of
"millers and bakers at fisticuffs." Most beautiful picture of
all, he sees them travelling schoolward by the late moon-
light which now and again in the winter months precedes
the tardy dawn.

That vision strikes me as being poetically true as well
as delightful: by which I mean that it is not sentimental:
we know that it ought to be true, that in a world well-
ordered according to our best wishes for it, it would be
naturally true. It expresses the natural love of Age,
brooding on the natural eager joy of children. But that
natural eager joy is just what our schools, in the matter
of reading, conscientiously kill.

In this matter of reading—of children's reading—
we stand, just now, or halt just now, between two ways.
The parent, I believe, has decisively won back to the
right one which good mothers never quite forsook.
There was an interval, lasting from the early years of

the last century until midway in Queen Victoria's reign
and a little beyond, when children were mainly brought
up on the assumption of natural vice. They might
adore father and mother, and yearn to be better friends
with papa: but there was the old Adam, a quickening
evil spirit; there were his imps always in the way, confound them! I myself lived, with excellent grand-
parents, for several years on pretty close terms with
Hell and an all-seeing Eye; until I grew so utterly weary
of both that I have never since had the smallest use for
either. Some of you may have read, as a curious book,
the agreeable history called *The Fairchild Family*, in
which Mr. Fairchild leads his naughty children afield to
a gallows by a cross-road and seating them under the
swinging corpse of a malefactor, deduces how easily
they may come to this if they go on as they have been
going. The authors of such monitory or cautionary
tales understood but one form of development, the
development of Original Sin. You stole a pin, and pro-
ceeded by fatal steps, to the penitentiary; you threw a
stick at a pheasant, turned poacher, shot a gamekeeper,
and ended on the gallows. You were always Eric and
it was always Little by Little with you. . . . Stay!
memory preserves one gem from a Sunday-school
dialogue, one sharp-cut intaglio of childhood springing
fully armed from the head of Satan:

    Q. Where hast thou been this Sabbath morning?
    A. I have been coursing of the squirrel.
    Q. Art not afraid so to desecrate the Lord's Day with
idle sport?

A. By no means: for I should tell you that I am an Atheist.

I forget what happened to that boy: but doubtless it was, as it should have been, something drastic.

The spell of prohibition, of repression, lies so strong upon these authors that when they try to break away from it, to appeal to something better than fear in the child, and essay to amuse, they become merely silly. For an example in verse:

> If Human Beings only knew
> What sorrows little birds go through,
>   I think that even boys
> Would never think it sport or fun
> To stand and fire a frightful gun
>   For nothing but the noise.

For another (instructional and quite a good *memoria technica* so far as it goes):

> William and Mary came next to the throne:
> When Mary died, there was William alone.

Now for a story of incident.—It comes from the book *Reading Without Tears*, that made my small sister weep. She did not weep over the story, because she did not claim to be an angel.

Did you ever hear of the donkey that went into the sea with the little cart? . . . A lady drove the cart down to the beach. She had six children with her. Three little ones sat in the cart by her side. Three bigger girls ran before the cart. When they came to the beach the lady and the children got out.

Very good so far. It opens like the story of Nausicäa [*Odyssey*, Book VI, lines 81–86].

The lady wished the donkey to bathe its legs in the sea, to make it strong and clean. But the donkey did not like to go near the sea. So the lady bound a brown shawl over its eyes, and she bade the big girls lead it close to the waves. Suddenly a big wave rushed to the land. The girls started back to avoid the wave, and they let go the donkey's rein.

The donkey was alarmed by the noise the girls made, and it went into the sea, not knowing where it was going because it was not able to see. The girls ran screaming to the lady, crying out, "The donkey is in the sea!"

There it was, going further and further into the sea, till the cart was hidden by the billows. The donkey sank lower and lower every moment, till no part of it was seen but the ears; for the brown shawl was over its nose and mouth. Now the children began to bawl and to bellow! But no one halloed so loud as the little boy of four. His name was Merty. He feared that the donkey was drowned. . . .

Two fishermen were in a boat far away. They said, "We hear howls and shrieks on the shore. Perhaps a boy or girl is drowning. Let us go and save him." So they rowed hard, and they soon came to the poor donkey, and saw its ears peeping out of the sea. The donkey was just going to sink when they lifted it up by the jaws, and seized the bridle and dragged it along. The children on the shore shouted aloud for joy. The donkey with the cart came safe to land. The poor creature was weak and dripping wet. The fishermen unbound its eyes, and said to the lady, "We cannot think how this thing came to be over its eyes." The lady said she wished she had not bound up its eyes, and she gave the shillings in her purse to the fishermen who had saved her donkey.

Now every child knows that a donkey may change into a Fairy Prince: that is a truth of imagination. But to be polite and say nothing of the lady, every child knows that no donkey would be ass enough to behave as in this narrative. And the good parents who, throughout the later eighteenth century and the nineteenth, inflicted this stuff upon children, were sinning against the light. Perrault's Fairy Tales, and Madame D'Aulnoy's were to their hand in translations; *Le Cabinet des Fées*, which includes these and M. Gulland's *Arabian Nights* and many another collection of delectable stories, extends on my shelves to forty-one volumes (the last volume appeared during the fury of the French Revolution!). The brothers Grimm published the first volume of their immortal tales in 1812, the second in 1814. A capital selection from them, charmingly rendered, was edited by our Edgar Taylor in 1823; and drew from Sir Walter Scott a letter of which some sentences are worth our pondering.

He writes:

There is also a sort of wild fairy interest in [these tales] which makes me think them fully better adapted to awaken the imagination and soften the heart of childhood than the good-boy stories which have been in later years composed for them. In the latter case their minds are, as it were, put into the stocks . . . and the moral always consists in good moral conduct being crowned with temporal success. Truth is, I would not give one tear shed over Little Red Riding Hood for all the benefit to be derived from a hundred histories of Jemmy Goodchild.

Few nowadays, I doubt, remember Gammer Grethel. She has been ousted by completer, maybe far better, translations of the Grimm's *Household Tales*. But turning back, the other day, to the old volume for the old sake's sake (as we say in the West) I came on the Preface—no child troubles with a Preface—and on these wise words:

> Much might be urged against that too rigid and philosophic (we might rather say, unphilosophic) exclusion of works of fancy and fiction from the libraries of children which is advocated by some. Our imagination is surely as susceptible of improvement by exercise as our judgment or our memory.

And that admirable sentence, Gentlemen, is the real text of my discourse to-day. I lay no sentimental stress upon Wordsworth's Ode and its doctrine that "Heaven lies about us in our infancy." It was, as you know, a favourite doctrine with our Platonists of the seventeenth century: and critics who trace back the Ode *Intimations of Immortality* to Henry Vaughan's

> Happy those early days, when I
> Shined in my Angel-infancy.

might connect it with a dozen passages from authors of that century. Here is one from *Centuries of Meditations* by that poor Welsh parson, Thomas Traherne whom I quoted to you the other day:

> Those pure and virgin apprehensions I had from the womb, and that divine light wherewith I was born are the best unto this day, wherein I can see the Universe. By the Gift of God they attended me into the world, and by His

4

special favour I remember them till now. . . . Certainly
Adam in Paradise had not more sweet and curious apprehensions of the world, than I when I was a child.

And here is another from John Earle's Character of
"A Child" in his *Microcosmography:*

His father hath writ him as his own little story, wherein
he reads those days of his life that he cannot remember; and
sighs to see what innocence he has out-liv'd.

He is the Christian's example, and the old man's relapse:
the one imitates his pureness, and the other falls into his
simplicity. Could he put off his body with his little coat,
he had got Eternity without a burthen, and exchang'd but
one Heaven for another.

Bethinking me again of "the small apple-eating urchin
whom we know," I suspect an amiable fallacy in all
this: I doubt if when he scales an apple-bearing tree
which is neither his own nor his papa's he does so under
impulse of any conscious yearning back to Hierusalem,
his happy home,

> Where trees for evermore bear fruit.

At any rate, I have an orchard, and he has put up
many excuses, but never yet that he was remembering
Sion.

Still the doctrine holds affinity with the belief which
I firmly hold and tried to explain to you with persuasion
last term: that, boy or man, you and I, the microcosms,
do—sensibly, half-sensibly, or insensibly—yearn,
through what we feel to be best in us, to "join up" with

the greater harmony; that by poetry or religion or what-
not we have that within us which craves to be drawn
out, "e-ducated," and linked up.

Now the rule of the nursery in the last century rested
on Original Sin, and consequently and quite logically
tended not to educate, but to repress. There are no new
fairy-tales of the days when your grandmothers wore
crinolines—I know, for I have searched. Mothers and
nurses taught the old ones; the Three Bears still found,
one after another, that "somebody has been sleeping in
my bed"; Fatima continued to call, "Sister Anne, do
you see any one coming?" the Wolf to show her teeth
under her nightcap and snarl out (O, great moment!),
"All the better to eat you with, my dear." But the
Evangelicals held the field. Those of our grandfathers
and grandmothers who understood joy and must have
had fairies for ministers—those of our grandmothers
who played croquet through a hoop with a bell and
practised Cupid's own sport of archery, those of our
grandfathers who wore jolly peg-top trousers and
Dundreary whiskers, and built the Crystal Palace and
drove to the Derby in green-veiled top-hats with Dutch
dolls stuck about the brim—*tot circa unum caput tumultuantes deos*—and those splendid uncles who used to
descend on the old school in a shower of gold—half-a-
sovereign at the very least—all these should have trailed
fairies with them in a cloud. But in practice the evan-
gelical parent held the majority, put away all toys
but Noah's Ark on Sundays, and voted the fairies down.

I know not who converted the parents. It may have

been that benefactor of Europe, Hans Christian Andersen, born at Odensee in Denmark, in April, 1805. He died, near Copenhagen, in 1875, having by a few months outlived his seventieth birthday. I like to think that his genius, a continuing influence over a long generation, did more than anything else to convert the parents. The schools, always more royalist than the King, professionally bleak, professionally dull, professionally repressive rather than educative, held on to a tradition which, though it had to be on the sly, every intelligent mother and nurse had done her best to evade. The schools made a boy's life penitential on a system. They discovered athletics, as a safety-valve for high spirits they could not cope with, and promptly made that safety-valve compulsory! They went on to make athletics a religion. Now athletics are not properly a religious exercise, and their meaning evaporates as soon as you enlist them in the service of repression. They are being used to do the exact opposite of that for which God meant them. Things are better now: but in those times how many a boy, having long looked forward to it, rejoiced in his last day at school?

I know surely enough what must be in your minds at this point: I am running up my head hard against the doctrine of Original Sin, against the doctrine that in dealing with a child you are dealing with a "fallen nature," with a human soul "conceived in sin," unregenerate except by repression; and therefore that repression and more repression *must* be the only logical way with your Original Sinners.

Well, then, I am. I have loved children all my life;
studied them in the nursery, studied them for years—
ten or twelve years intimately—in elementary schools.
I know for a surety, if I have acquired any knowledge,
that the child is a "child of God" rather than a "child
of wrath"; and here before you I proclaim that to connect in any child's mind the Book of Joshua with the
Gospels, to make its Jehovah identical in that young
mind with the Father of Mercy of whom Jesus was the
Son, to confuse, as we do in any school in this land between 9.5 and 9.45 A.M., the bloodthirsty tribal deity
whom the Hohenzollern family invokes with the true
God the Father, is a blasphemous usage, and a curse.

But let me get away to milder heresies. If you will
concede for a moment that the better way with a child
is to draw out, to *educate*, rather than to repress, what is
in him, let us observe what he instinctively wants. Now
first, of course, he wants to eat and drink, and to run
about. When he passes beyond these merely animal
desires to what we may call the instinct of growth in his
soul, how does he proceed. I think Mr. Holmes, whom
I have already quoted, very fairly sets out these desires
as any grown-up person can perceive them. The child
desires

    (1) to talk and to listen;
    (2) to act (in the dramatic sense of the word);
    (3) to draw, paint, and model;
    (4) to dance and sing;
    (5) to know the why of things;
    (6) to construct things.

Now I shall have something to say by and by on the
amazing preponderance in this list of those instincts
which Aristotle would have called *mimetic*. This morning I take only the least imitative of all, the desire to
know the why of things.

Surely you know, taking only this, that the master-
key admitting a child to all, or almost all, palaces of
knowledge is his ability to *read*. When he has grasped
that key of his mother-tongue he can with perseverance
unlock all doors to all the avenues of knowledge. More
—he has the passport to heavens unguessed.

You will perceive at once that what I mean here by
"reading" is the capacity for silent reading, taking a
book apart and mastering it; and you will bear in mind
the wonder that I preached to you in a previous lecture
—that great literature never condescends, that what
yonder boy in a corner reads of a king is happening
to *him*. Do you suppose that in an elementary school
one child in ten reads thus? Listen to a wise ex-inspect-
or, whose words I can corroborate of experience:

The first thing that strikes the visitor who enters an
ordinary elementary school while a reading lesson is in
progress is that the children are not reading at all, in the
accepted sense of the word. They are not reading to themselves, not studying, not mastering the contents of the book,
not assimilating the mental and spiritual nutriment that it
may be supposed to contain. They are standing up one by
one and reading aloud to their teacher.

Ah! but I have seen far worse than that. I have visited
and condemned rural schools where the practice was to

stand a class up—say a class of thirty children—and make them read in unison: which meant, of course, that the front row chanted out the lesson while the back rows made inarticulate noises. I well remember one such exhibition, in a remote country school on the Cornish hills, and having my attention arrested midway by the face of a girl in the third row. She was a strikingly beautiful child, with that combination of bright auburn, almost flaming, hair with dark eyebrows, dark eyelashes, dark eyes, which of itself arrests your gaze being so rare; and those eyes seemed to challenge me half scornfully and ask, "Are you really taken in by all this?" Well, I soon stopped the performance and required each child to read separately: whereupon it turned out that, in the upper standards of this school of seventy or eighty children, one only—this disdainful girl—could get through half a dozen easy sentences with credit. She read well and intelligently, being accustomed to read to herself, at home.

I daresay that this bad old method of block-reading is dead by this time.

Reading aloud and *separately* is excellent for several purposes. It tests capacity: it teaches correct pronunciation by practice, as well as the mastery of difficult words: it provides a good teacher with frequent opportunities of helping the child to understand what he reads.

But as his schooling proceeds he should be accustomed more and more to read to himself: for that, I repeat, is the master key.

CHILDREN'S READING (II)

I

IN our talk, Gentlemen, about Children's Reading we left off upon a list, drawn up by Mr. Holmes in his book *What Is, and What Might Be*, of the things that, apart from physical nourishment and exercise, a child instinctively desires.

(1) to talk and to listen;
(2) to act (in the dramatic sense of the word);
(3) to draw, paint, and model;
(4) to dance and sing;
(5) to know the why of things;
(6) to construct things.

Let us scan through this catalogue briefly, in its order.

No. (1). *To talk and to listen*—Mr. Holmes calls this *the communicative instinct*. Every child wants to talk, with those about him, or at any rate with his chosen ones—his parents, brothers, sisters, nurse, governess, gardener, boot-boy (if he possess these last)—with other children, even if his dear papa is poor: to tell them what he has been doing, seeing, feeling: and to listen to what they have to tell him.

Nos. (2), (3), (4). *To act*—our author calls this the

"dramatic instinct": *to draw, paint, and model*—this the "artistic instinct": *to dance and sing*—this the "musical instinct." But obviously all these are what Aristotle would call "mimetic" instincts: "imitative" (in a sense I shall presently explain); even as No. (2)—acting— like No. (1)—talking and listening—comes of craving for sympathy. In fact, as we go on, you will see that these instincts overlap and are not strictly separable, though we separate them just now for convenience.

No. (5). *To know the why of things*—the "inquisitive instinct." This, being the one which gives most trouble to parents, parsons, governesses, conventional schoolmasters—to all grown-up persons who pretend to know what they don't and are ashamed to tell what they do— is of course the most ruthlessly repressed.

> "The time is come," the Infant said,
>   "To talk of many things:
>   Of babies, storks and cabbages
>   And—

—having studied the Evangelists' Window facing the family pew—

> And whether cows have wings."

The answer, in my experience, is invariably stern, and "in the negative": in tolerant moments compromising on "Wait, like a good boy, and see."

But we singled out this instinct and discussed it in our last lecture.

No. (6). *To construct things*—the "constructive instinct." I quote Mr. Holmes here:

After analysis comes synthesis. The child pulls his toys to pieces in order that he may, if possible, reconstruct them. The ends that he sets before himself are those which Comte set before the human race—*savoir pour prévoir, afin de pouvoir: induire pour déduire, afin de construire.* The desire to make things, to build things up, to control ways and means, to master the resources of nature, to put his knowledge of her laws and facts to practical use, is strong in his soul. Give him a box of bricks, and he will spend hours in building and rebuilding houses, churches. . . . Set him on a sandy shore with a spade and a pail, and he will spend hours in constructing fortified castles with deep encircling moats.

Again, obviously, this constructive instinct overlaps with the imitative ones. Construction, for example, enters into the art of making mud-pies and has also been applied in the past to great poetry. If you don't keep a sharp eye in directing this instinct, it may conceivably end in an *Othello* or in a *Divina Commedia*.

II

Without preaching on any of the others, however, I take three of the six instincts scheduled by Mr. Holmes —the three which you will allow to be almost purely imitative. They are:

Acting,

Drawing, painting, modelling,

Dancing and singing.

Now let us turn to the very first page of Aristotle's *Poetics* and what do we read?

Epic poetry and Tragedy, Comedy also and dithyrambic poetry, and the greater part of the music of the flute and of the lyre, are all, in general, modes of imitation. . . .

For as there are persons who represent a number of things by colours and drawings, and others vocally, so it is with the arts above mentioned. They all imitate by rhythm, language, harmony, singly or combined.

Even dancing (he goes on)

imitates character, emotion, and action, by rhythmical movement.

Now, having touched on mud-pies, let me say a few words upon these æsthetic imitative instincts of acting, dancing, singing before I follow Aristotle into his explanation of the origin of Poetry, which I think we may agree to be the highest subject of our Art of Reading and to hold promise of its highest reward.

Every wise mother sings or croons to her child and dances him on her knee. She does so by sure instinct, long before the small body can respond or his eyes— always blue at first and unfathomably aged—return her any answer. It lulls him into the long spells of sleep so necessary for his first growth. By and by, when he has found his legs, he begins to skip, and even before he has found articulate speech, to croon for himself. Pass a stage, and you find him importing speech, drama, dance, incantation, into his games with his playmates. Watch a cluster of children as they enact *"Here we go gathering nuts in May"*—eloquent line: it is just what they are doing!—or *"Here come three Dukes a-riding,"* or *"Fetch a pail of water,"* or *"Sally, Sally Waters"*:

> Sally, Sally Waters,
>   Sitting in the sand,
> Rise, Sally—rise, Sally,
>   For a young man.

Suitor presented, accepted [I have noted, by the way, that this game is more popular with girls than with boys]; wedding ceremony hastily performed—so hastily, it were more descriptive to say "taken for granted"— within the circle; the dancers, who join hands and resume the measure, chanting

> Now you are married, we wish you joy—
>   First a girl and then a boy

—the order, I suspect, dictated by exigencies of rhyme rather than of Eugenics, as Dryden confessed that a rhyme had often helped him to a thought. And yet I don't know; for the incantation goes on to redress the balance in a way that looks scientific:

> Ten years after, son and daughter,
> And now—

[practically!]

> And now, Miss Sally, come out of the water.

The players end by supplying the applause which, in these days of division of labour, is commonly left to the audience.

III

Well, there you have it all: acting, singing, dancing, choral movement—enlisted ancillary to the domestic drama: and, when you start collecting evidence of these imitative instincts blent in childhood the mass will soon amaze you and leave you no room to be surprised that many learned scholars, on the supposition that un-civilised man is a child more or less—and at least so much of child that one can argue through children's practice to his—have found the historical origin of Poetry itself in these primitive performances: "com-munal poetry" as they call it. I propose to discuss with you (maybe next term) in a lecture not belonging to this "course" the likelihood that what we call specifi-cally "the Ballad," or "Ballad Poetry," originated thus. Here is a wider question. Did all Poetry de-velope out of this, historically, as a process in time and in fact? These scholars (among whom I will instance one of the most learned—Dr. Gummere) hold that it did: and I may take a passage from Dr. Gummere's *Beginnings of Poetry* (p. 95) to show you how they call in the practice of savage races to support their theory. The Botocudos of South America are—according to Dr. Paul Ehrenreich who has observed them[1]—an un-gentlemanly tribe, "very low in the social scale."

The Botocudos are little better than a leaderless horde, and pay scant respect to their chieftain; they live only for their immediate bodily needs, and take small thought for

[1] The reference given is *Zeitschr. f. Ethnologie*, xix., 30 ff.

the morrow, still less for the past. No traditions, no legends,
are abroad to tell them of their forbears. They still use
gestures to express feeling and ideas; while the number of
words which imitate a given sound "is extraordinarily
great." An action or an object is named by imitating the
sound peculiar to it; and sounds are doubled to express
greater intensity. . . . To speak is *aō;* to speak loudly or
to sing, is *aō-aō*. And now for their æsthetic life, their song,
dance, poetry, as described by this accurate observer. "On
festal occasions the whole horde meets by night round the
camp fire for a dance. Men and women alternating . . .
form a circle; each dancer lays his arms about the necks of
his two neighbours, and the entire ring begins to turn to the
right or to the left, while all the dancers stamp strongly and
in rhythm the foot that is advanced, and drag after it the
other foot. Now with drooping heads they press closer and
closer together; now they widen the circle. Throughout
the dance resounds a monotonous song to which they stamp
their feet. Often one can hear nothing but a continually
repeated *Kalauī ahā!* . . . Again, however, short improvised songs, in which we are told the doings of the day, the
reasons for rejoicing, what not, as "Good hunting," or
"Now we have something to eat," or "Brandy is good."

"As to the æsthetic value" of these South American
utterances, Dr. Gummere asks in a footnote, "how far is
it inferior to the sonorous commonplaces of our own
verse—say *The Psalm of Life?*" I really cannot answer
that question. Which do you prefer, Gentlemen?—
"Life is real, life is earnest," or "Now we have something to eat." I must leave you to settle it with the
Food Controller.

The Professor goes on:

"Now and then, too, an individual begins a song, and is
answered by the rest in chorus. . . . *They never sing with-*

out dancing, never dance without singing, and have but one word to express both song and dance."

As the unprejudiced reader sees [Dr. Gummere proceeds] this clear and admirable account confirms the doctrine of early days revived with fresh ethnological evidence in the writings of Dr. Brown and of Adam Smith, that dance, poetry, and song were once a single and inseparable function, and is in itself fatal to the idea of rhythmic prose, of solitary recitation, as foundations of poetry. . . . All poetry is communal, holding fast to the rhythm of consent as to the one sure fact.

IV

Now I should tell you, Gentlemen, that I hold such utterances as this last—whatever you may think of the utterances of the Botocudos—to be exorbitant: that I distrust all attempts to build up (say) *Paradise Lost* historically from the yells and capers of recondite savages. "Life is real, life is earnest" may be no better æsthetically (I myself think it a little better) than "Now we have something to eat." "Brandy is good" may rival Pindar's "Ἄριστον μὲν ὕδωρ and indeed puts what it contains of truth with more of finality, less of provocation (though Pindar at once follows up "Ἄριστον μὲν ὕδωρ with exquisite poetry): but you cannot—truly you cannot—exhibit the steps which lead up from "Brandy is good" to such lines as

> Thus with the year
> Seasons return; but not to me returns
> Day, or the sweet approach of even or morn,
> Or sight of vernal bloom, or summer's rose,
> Or flocks, or herds, or human face divine.

I bend over the learned page pensively, and I seem to see a Botocudo Professor—though not high "in the social scale," they may have such things—visiting Cambridge on the last night of the Lent races and reporting of its inhabitants as follows:

They pay scant heed to their chiefs: they live only for their immediate bodily needs, and take small thought for the morrow. On festal occasions the whole horde meets by night round the camp fire for a dance. Each dancer lays his arms about the necks of his two neighbours, stamping strongly with one foot and dragging the other after it. Now with drooping heads they press closer and closer together; now they widen the circle. Often one can hear nothing but a continually repeated *kalauī ahā*, or again one hears short improvised songs in which we are told the doings of the day, the reasons for rejoicing, what not, as "Good hunting," "Good old—"[naming a tribal God], or in former times "*Now* we shall be but a short while," or "*Wōemma!*" Now and then, too, an individual begins a song and is answered by the rest in chorus—such as

> For he is an estimable person
> Beyond possibility of gainsaying.

The chorus twice repeats this and asseverates that they are following a custom common to the flotilla, the expeditionary force, and even their rude seats of learning.

And Dr. Gummere, or somebody else, comments: "As the unprejudiced reader will see, this clear and admirable account confirms our hypothesis that in communal celebration we have at once the origin and model of two poems, *Paradise Lost* and *In Memoriam*, recorded as having been composed by members of this very tribe."

Although we have been talking of instincts, we are

not concerned here with the steps by which the child, or the savage, following an instinct attains to *write* poetry; but, more modestly, with the instinct by which the child *likes* it, and the way in which he can be best encouraged to read and improve this natural liking. Nor are we even concerned here to define Poetry. It suffices our present purpose to consider Poetry as the sort of thing the poets write.

But obviously if we find a philosopher discussing poetry without any reference to children, and independently basing it upon the very same imitative instincts which we have noted in children, we have some promise of being on the right track.

V

So I return to Aristotle. Aristotle (I shall in fairness say) does not anticipate Dr. Gummere, to contradict or refute him; he may even be held to support him incidentally. But he sticks to business, and this is what he says (*Poetics*, c. iv.):

Poetry in general seems to have sprung from two causes, and these natural causes. First the instinct to imitate is implanted in man from his childhood, and in this he differs from other animals, being the most imitative of them all. Man gets his first learning through imitation, and all men delight in seeing things imitated. This is clearly shown by experience. . . .

To imitate, then, being instinctive in our nature, so too we have an instinct for harmony and rhythm, metre being manifestly a species of rhythm: and man, being born to these instincts and little by little improving them, out of his early improvisations created Poetry.

Combining these two instincts, with him, we arrive
at *harmonious imitation*. Well and good. But what is
it we imitate in poetry?—noble things or mean things?
After considering this, putting mean things aside as
unworthy, and voting for the nobler—which must at
the same time be true, since without truth there can
be no real nobility—Aristotle has to ask "In what way
true? True to ordinary life, with its observed defeats
of the right by the wrong? or true, as again instinct tells
good men it should be, *universally?*" So he arrives at
his conclusion that a true thing is not necessarily truth
of fact in a world where truth in fact is so often belied
or made meaningless—not the record that Alcibiades
went somewhere and suffered something—but truth to
the Universal, the superior demand of our conscience.
In such a way only we know that *The Tempest* or *Paradise Lost* or *The Ancient Mariner* or *Prometheus Unbound* can be truer than any police report. Yet we
know that they are truer in essence, and in significance,
since they appeal to eternal verities—since they imitate
the Universal—whereas the police report chronicles
(faithfully, as in duty bound, even usefully in its way)
events which may, nay must, be significant somehow
but cannot at best be better to us than phenomena,
broken ends, and shards.

VI

I return to the child. Clearly in obeying the instinct
which I have tried to illustrate, he is searching to realize

himself; and, as educators, we ought to help this effort
—or, at least, not to hinder it.

Further, if we agree with Aristotle, in this searching
to realize himself through imitation, what will the child
most nobly and naturally imitate? He will imitate what
Aristotle calls "the Universal," the superior demand.
And does not this bring us back to consent with what I
have been preaching from the start in this course—that
to realize ourselves in *What Is* not only in degree transcends mere knowledge and activity, *What Knows* and
What Does, but transcends it in kind? It is not only
what the child unconsciously longs for: it is that for
which (in St. Paul's words) "the whole creation groan-
eth and travaileth in pain together until now"; craving
for this (I make you the admission) as emotionally as
the heart may be thrilled, the breast surge, the eyes
swell with tears, at a note drawn from the violin: feeling
that somewhere, beyond reach, we have a lost sister,
and she speaks to our soul.

VII

Who, that has been a child, has not felt this surprise
of beauty, the revelation, the call of it?

> The sounding cataract
> Haunted me like a passion . . .

—yes, or a rainbow on the spray against a cliff; or a vista
of lawns between descending woods; or a vision of fish
moving in a pool under the hazel's shadow? Who has

not felt the small surcharged heart labouring with desire
to express it?

I preach to you that the base of all Literature, of all
Poetry, of all Theology, is one, and stands on one rock:
*the very highest Universal Truth is something so simple
that a child may understand it.* This surely, was in
Jesus' mind when he said, "I thank thee, O Father, Lord
of heaven and earth, because thou hast hid these things
from the wise and prudent, and hast revealed them unto
babes."

For as the Universe is one, so the individual human
souls, that apprehend it, have no varying values intrin-
sically, but one equal value. They vary but in power to
apprehend, and this may be more easily hindered than
helped by the conceit begotten of finite knowledge. I
shall even dare to quote of this Universal Truth, the
words I once hardily put into the mouth of John Wesley
concerning divine Love: "I see now that if God's love
reach up to every star and down to every poor soul on
earth, it must be vastly simple; so simple that all dwel-
lers on Earth may be assured of it—as all who have eyes
may be assured of the planet shining yonder at the end
of the street—and so vast that all bargaining is below
it, and they may inherit it without considering his
deserts." I believe this to be strictly and equally true
of the appeal which Poetry makes to each of us, child
or man, in his degree. As Johnson said of Gray's *Elegy*,
it "abounds with images which find a mirror in every
mind, and with sentiments to which every bosom returns an echo." It exalts us through the best of us, by

telling us something new yet not strange, something that we *recognize*, something that we, too, have known, or surmised, but had never the delivering speech to tell. "There is a pleasure in poetic pains," says Wordsworth: but, Gentlemen, if you have never felt the travail, yet you have still to understand the bliss of deliverance.

VIII

If, then, you consent with me thus far in theory, let us now drive at practice. You have (we will say) a class of thirty or forty in front of you. We will assume that they know their *a—b*, *ab*, can at least spell out their words. You will choose a passage for them, and you will not (if you are wise) choose a passage from *Paradise Lost:* your knowledge telling you that *Paradise Lost* was written, late in his life, by a great *virtuoso*, and older men (of whom I, sad to say, am one) assuring you that to taste the Milton of *Paradise Lost* a man must have passed his thirtieth year. You take the early Milton: you read out this, for instance, from *L'Allegro:*

> Haste thee, Nymph, and bring with thee
> Jest and youthful Jollity,
> Quips, and Cranks, and wanton wiles,
> Nods and Becks, and wreathed Smiles
> Such as hang on Hebe's cheek,
> And love to live in dimple sleek;
> Sport that wrinkled Care derides,
> And Laughter holding both his sides. . . .

Go on: just read it to them. They won't know who Hebe was, but you can tell them later. The metre is

taking hold of them (in my experience the metre of
L'Allegro can be relied upon to grip children) and
anyway they can see "Laughter holding both his sides":
they recognize it as if they saw the picture. Go on
steadily:

> Come, and trip it as ye go,
> On the light fantastick toe;
> And in thy right hand lead with thee
> The Mountain Nymph, sweet Liberty;
> And, if I give thee honour due,
> Mirth, admit me of thy crew—

Do not pause and explain what a Nymph is, or why
Liberty is the "Mountain Nymph!" Go on reading:
the Prince has always to break through briers to kiss
the Sleeping Beauty awake. Go on with the incantation
calling him, persuading him, that he is the Prince and
she is worth it. Go on reading—

> Mirth, admit me of thy crew,
> To live with her, and live with thee,
> In unreprovéd pleasures free;
> To hear the lark begin his flight,
> And singing startle the dull night,
> From his watch-towre in the skies,
> Till the dappled dawn doth rise.

At this point—still as you read without stopping to
explain, the child certainly feels that he is being led to
something. He knows the lark: but the lark's "watch-
towre"—he had never thought of that: and "the dap-
pled dawn"—yes that's just *it*, now he comes to think:

Then to come, in spite of sorrow,
And at my window bid good-morrow,
Through the sweet-brier or the vine
Or the twisted eglantine;
While the cock with lively din
Scatters the rear of Darkness thin;
And to the stack, or the barn door
Stoutly struts his dames before:
Oft listening how the hounds and horn
Cheerily rouse the slumbering Morn,
From the side of some hoar hill,
Through the high wood echoing shrill:
Sometime walking, not unseen,
By hedgerow elms on hillocks green,
Right against the eastern gate,
Where the great sun begins his state,
Robed in flames and amber light,
The clouds in thousand liveries dight;
While the ploughman, near at hand,
Whistles o'er the furrow'd land,
And the milkmaid singeth blithe,
And the mower whets his sithe,
And every shepherd tells his tale
Under the hawthorn in the dale.

Don't stop (I say) to explain that Hebe was (for once) the legitimate daughter of Zeus and, as such, had the privilege to draw wine for the gods. Don't even stop, just yet, to explain who the gods were. Don't discourse on amber, otherwise ambergris; don't explain that "gris" in this connection doesn't mean "grease"; don't trace it through the Arabic into Noah's Ark; don't prove its electrical properties by tearing up paper into little bits and attracting them with the mouth-piece of your pipe rubbed on your sleeve. Don't insist philologically that when every shepherd "tells his tale" he is not relating an anecdote but simply keeping tally of his flock.

Just go on reading, as well as you can; and be sure that when the children get the thrill of it, for which you wait, they will be asking more questions, and pertinent ones, than you are able to answer.

IX

This advice, to be sure, presupposes of the teacher himself some capacity of reading aloud, and reading aloud is not taught in our schools. In our Elementary Schools, in which few of the pupils contemplate being called to Holy Orders or to the Bar, it is practised, indeed, but seldom taught as an art. In our Secondary and Public Schools it is neither taught nor practised: as I know to my cost—and you, to yours, Gentlemen, on whom I have had to practise.

But let the teacher take courage. First let him read a passage "at the long breath"—as the French say— aloud, and persuasively as he can. Now and then he may pause to indicate some particular beauty, repeating the line before he proceeds. But he should be sparing of these interruptions. When Laughter, for example, is already "holding both his sides" it cannot be less than officious, a work of supererogation, to stop and hold them for him; and he who obeys the counsel of perfection will read straight to the end and then recur to particular beauties. Next let him put up a child to continue with the tale, and another and another, just as in a construing class. While the boy is reading, the teacher should *never* interrupt: he should wait, and return afterwards upon a line that has been slurred or wrongly emphasised. When the children have done reading he should invite questions on any point they have found puzzling: it is with the operation of poetry on *their* minds that his main business lies. Lastly, he may run back over significant points they have missed.

"And is that all the method?"—Yes, that is all the method. "So simple as that?"—Yes, even so simple as that, and (I claim) even so wise, seeing that it just lets the author—Chaucer or Shakespeare or Milton or Coleridge—have his own way with the young plant —just lets them drop "like the gentle rain from heaven," and soak in.

> The moving Moon went up the sky,
>   And nowhere did abide:
> Softly she was going up,
>   And a star or two beside.

Do you really want to chat about *that?* Cannot you trust it?

> The stars were dim, and thick the night,
> The steersman's face by his lamp gleamed white;
>   From the sails the dew did drip—
> Till clomb above the eastern bar
> The hornèd Moon, with one bright star
>   Within the nether tip.

Must you tell them that for the Moon to hold a star anywhere within her circumference is an astronomical impossibility? Very well, then; tell it. But tell it after-

wards, and put it away quietly. For the quality of
Poetry is not strained. Let the rain soak; then use your
hoe, and gently; and still trust Nature; by which, I
again repeat to you, all spirit attracts all spirit as inevitably as all matter attracts all matter.

"Strained." I am glad that memory flew just here
to the word of Portia's: for it carries me on to a wise
page of Dr. Corson's, and a passage in which, protesting
against the philologers who cram our children's handbooks with irrelevant information that but obscures
what Chaucer or Shakespeare *mean*, he breaks out in
Chaucer's own words:

> Thise cookes! how they stampe and streyne and grind,
> And turnen substaunce into accident!

(Yes, and make the accident the substance!)—as he
insists that the true subject of literary study is the
author's meaning; and the true method a surrender of
the mind to that meaning, with what Wordsworth calls
"a wise passiveness":

> The eye—it cannot choose but see;
> We cannot bid the ear be still;
> Our bodies feel, where'er they be,
> Against or with our will.
>
> Nor less I deem that there are Powers
> Which of themselves our minds impress;
> That we can feed this mind of ours
> In a wise passiveness.
>
> Think you, 'mid all this mighty sum
> Of things for ever speaking,
> That nothing of itself will come
> But we must still be seeking?

X

I have been talking to-day about children; and find
that most of the while I have been thinking, if but sub-
consciously, of poor children.   Now, at the end, you
may ask "Why, lecturing here at Cambridge, is he pre-
occupied with poor children who leave school at fourteen
and under, and thereafter read no poetry?" . . . Oh,
yes! I know all about these children and the hopeless,
wicked waste; these with a common living-room to
read in, a father tired after his day's work, and (for
parental encouragement) just the two words "Get out!"
A Scots domine writes in his log:

I have discovered a girl with a sense of humour.   I asked
my qualifying class to draw a graph of the attendance at a
village kirk.   "And you must explain away any rise or fall,"
I said.

Margaret Steel had a huge drop one Sunday, and her
explanation was "Special Collection for Missions."   Next
Sunday the Congregation was abnormally large: Margaret
wrote "Change of Minister." . . .   Poor Margaret! When
she is fourteen, she will go out into the fields, and in three
years she will be an ignorant country bumpkin.

And again:

Robert Campbell (a favourite pupil) left the school to-day.
He had reached the age-limit. . . .   Truly it is like death: I
stand by a new-made grave, and I have no hope of a resurrection.   Robert is dead.

Precisely because I have lived on close terms with
this, and the wicked waste of it, I appeal to you who

are so much more fortunate than this Robert or this
Margaret and will have far more to say in the world, to
think of them—how many they are. I am not senti-
mentalising. When an Elementary Schoolmaster
spreads himself and tells me he looks upon every child
entering his school as a potential Lord Chancellor, I
answer that, as I expect, so I should hope, to die before
seeing the world a Woolsack. Jack cannot ordinarily be
as good as his master; if he were, he would be a great
deal better. You have given Robert a vote, however,
and soon you will have to give it to Margaret. Can
you not give them also, in their short years at school,
something to sustain their souls in the long Valley of
Humiliation?

Do you remember this passage in *The Pilgrim's Progress*—as the pilgrims passed down that valley?

Now as they were going along and talking, they espied a
Boy feeding his Father's Sheep. The Boy was in very mean
Cloaths, but of a very fresh and well-favoured Countenance,
and as he sate by himself he Sung. Hark, said Mr. Great-
heart, to what the Shepherd's Boy saith.

Well, it was a very pretty song, about Contentment.

He that is down need fear no fall,
    He that is low, no Pride:
He that is humble ever shall
    Have God to be his Guide.

But I care less for its subject than for the song. Though
life condemn him to live it through in the Valley of
Humiliation, I want to hear the Shepherd Boy singing.

ON READING FOR EXAMINATIONS

I

YOU, Gentlemen, who so far have followed with patience this course of lectures, advertised, maybe too ambitiously, as "On the Art of Reading," will recall to your memory, when I challenge it across the intervals of Vacation, that three propositions have been pretty steadily held before you.

The *first:* (bear me out) that, man's life being of the length it is, and his activities multifarious as they are, out of the mass of printed matter already loaded and still being shot upon this planet, he *must* make selection. There is no other way.

The *second:* that—the time and opportunity being so brief, the mass so enormous, and the selection therefore so difficult—he should select the books that are best for him, and take them *absolutely*, not frittering his time upon books written about and around the best: that— in their order, of course—the primary masterpieces shall come first, and the secondary second, and so on; and mere chat about any of them last of all.

My *third* proposition (perhaps more discutable) has been that, the human soul's activities being separated, so far as we can separate them, into *What Does, What*

Knows, What Is—to *be* such-and-such a man ranks
higher than either *knowing* or *doing* this, that, or the
other: that it transcends all man's activity upon phenomena, even a Napoleon's: all his housed store of knowledge, though it be a Casaubon's or a Mark Pattison's:
that only by learning to *be* can we understand or reach,
as we have an instinct to reach, to our right place in the
scheme of things: and that, any way, all the greatest
literature commands this instinct.　To be Hamlet—to
feel yourself Hamlet—is more important than killing
a king or even knowing all there is to be known about
a text.　Now most of us have been Hamlet, more or less:
while few of us, I trust, have ever murdered a monarch:
and still fewer, perhaps, can hope to know all that is to
be known of the text of the play.　But for value, Gentlemen, let us not rank these three achievements by order
of their rarity.　Shakespeare means us to feel—to *be*—
Hamlet.　That is all: and from the play it is the best we
can get.

II

Now in talking to you, last term, about children I
had perforce to lay stress on the point that, with all this
glut of literature, the mass of children in our common-
wealth, who leave school at fourteen go forth starving.

But you are happier.　You are happier, not in having
your selection of reading in English done for you at
school (for you have in the Public Schools scarce any
such help): but happier (1) because the time of learning

is so largely prolonged, and (2) because this most difficult office of sorting out from the mass what you should read as most profitable has been tentatively performed for you by us older men for your relief. For example, those of you—"if any," as the Regulations say—who will, a week or two hence, be sitting for Section A of the Mediæval and Modern Languages Tripos, have been spared, all along, the laborious business of choosing what you should read or read with particular attention for the good of your souls. Is Chaucer your author? Then you will have read (or ought to have read) *The Parlement of Fowles*, the *Prologue* to The Canterbury Tales, *The Knight's Tale*, *The Man of Law's Tale*, *The Nun Priest's Tale*, *The Doctor's Tale*, *The Pardoner's Tale* with its Prologue, *The Friar's Tale*. You were not dissuaded from reading *Troilus;* you were not forbidden to read all the Canterbury Tales, even the naughtiest; but the works that I have mentioned have been "prescribed" for you. So, of Shakespeare, we do not discourage you (at all events, intentionally) from reading *Macbeth, Othello, As You Like It, The Tempest*, any play you wish. In other years we "set" each of these in its turn. But for this Year of Grace we insist upon *King John, The Merchant of Venice, King Henry IV, Part I, Much Ado about Nothing, Hamlet, King Lear*, "certain specified works"—and so on, with other courses of study. Why is this done? Be fair to us, Gentlemen. We do it not only to accommodate the burden to your backs, to avoid overtaxing one-and-a-half or two years of study; not merely to guide you that you do not dissipate your reading, that you shall—with us, at any rate—know where you are. We do it chiefly, and honestly—you likewise being honest—to give you each year, in each prescribed course, a sound nucleus of knowledge, out of which, later, your minds can reach to more. We are not, in the last instance, praiseworthy or blameworthy for your range. I think, perhaps, too little of a man's *range* in his short while here between (say) nineteen and twenty-two. For anything I care, the kernel may be as small as you please. To plant it wholesome, for a while tend to it wholesome, then to show it the sky and that it is wide—not a hot-house, nor a brassy cupola over a man, but an atmosphere shining up league on league; to reach the moment of saying, "All this now is yours, if you have the perseverance as I have taught you the power, *coelum nactus es, hoc exorna*": this, even in our present Tripos, we endeavour to do.

III

All very well. But, as Elizabeth Barrett Browning asked,

Do ye hear the children weeping, O my brothers?

"Yes," I hear you ingeminate; "but what about examinations? We thank you, sirs, for thus relieving and guiding us: we acknowledge your excellent intentions. But in practice you hang up a bachelor's gown and hood on a pole, and right under and just in front of it you

set the examination-barrier. For this in practice we run
during three years or so, and to this all the time you
are exhorting, directing us—whether you mean it or
not, though we suspect that you cannot help yourselves.
Yes; and, as labouring swimmers will turn their eyes
even to a little boat in the offing, I hear you pant, "This
man at all events—always so insistent that good literature teaches *What Is* rather than *What Knows*—will
bring word that we may float on our backs, bathe,
enjoy these waters and be refreshed, instead of striving
through them competitive for a goal. He *must* condemn
literary examinations, nine tenths of which treat Literature as matter of Knowledge merely."

IV

I am sorry, Gentlemen: I cannot bring you so much
of comfort as all that. I have a love of the past which,
because it goes down to the roots, has sometimes been
called Radicalism: I could never consent with Bacon's
gibe at antiquity as *pessimum conjurium*, and examinations have a very respectable antiquity. Indeed no university to my knowledge has ever been able in the long
run to do without them: and although certain colleges
—King's College and New College at Oxford—for long
persevered in the attempt, the result was not altogether happy, and in the end they have consigned to
custom.

Of course universities have experimented with the
process. Let me give you two or three ancient examples

6

which may help you to see (to vary Wordsworth) that
though "the Form decays, the function never dies."

(1) I begin with most ancient Bologna, famous for
Civil Law. At Bologna the process of graduation—of
admission to the *jus docendi*, "right to teach"—con-
sisted of two parts, the Private Examination and the
Public (*conventus*):

The private Examination was the real test of competence,
the so-called public Examination being in practice a mere
ceremony. Before admission to each of these tests the candidate was presented by the Consiliarius of his Nation to the
Rector for permission to enter it, and swore that he had
complied with all the statutable conditions, that he would
give no more than the statutable fees or entertainments to
the Rector himself, the Doctor, or his fellow-students, and
that he would obey the Rector. Within a period of eight
days before the Examination the candidate was presented
by "his own" Doctor or by some other Doctor or by two
Doctors to the Archdeacon, the presenting Doctor being
required to have satisfied himself by private examination of
his presentee's fitness. Early on the morning of the Examination, after attending a Mass of the Holy Ghost, the
candidate appeared before the assembled College and was
assigned by one of the Doctors present two passages (*puncta*)
in the Civil or Canon Law as the case might be. He then
retired to his house to study the passages, *in doing which it
would appear that he had the assistance of the presenting
Doctor*. Later in the day the Doctors were summoned to
the Cathedral, or some other public building, by the Archdeacon, who presided over but took no active part in the
ensuing examination. The candidate was then introduced
to the Archdeacon and Doctors by the presenting Doctor or
Promoter as he was styled. The Prior of the College then
administered a number of oaths in which the candidate
promised respect to that body and solemnly renounced all

the rights of which the College had succeeded in robbing all Doctors of other Colleges not included in its ranks.   The candidate then gave a lecture or exposition of the two prepared passages: after which he was examined upon them by two of the Doctors appointed by the College.   Other Doctors might ask supplementary questions of Law (which they were required to swear that they had not previously communicated to the candidate) arising more indirectly out of the passages selected, or might suggest objections to the answers.   With a tender regard for the feelings of their comrades at this "rigorous and tremendous Examination" (as they style it) the Statutes required the Examiner to treat the examinee as *his own son.*

But, knowing what we do of parental discipline in the Middle Ages, we need not take this to enjoin a weak excess of leniency.

The Examination concluded, the votes of the Doctors present were taken by ballot and the candidate's fate determined by the majority, the decision being announced by the Archdeacon.

(2) Let us pass to the great and famous University of Paris.   At Paris,

In 1275, if not earlier, a preliminary test (or "Responsions") was instituted to ascertain the fitness of those who wanted to take part in the public performance.   At these "Responsions" which took place in the December before the Lent in which the candidate was to determine, he had to dispute in Grammar and Logic with a Master.   If this test was passed in a satisfactory manner, the candidate was admitted to the *Examen Baccalariandorum,* Examination for the Baccalaureate, which was conducted by a board of Examiners appointed by each Nation for its own candidates.

The duty of the Examiners was twofold, firstly to ascertain by inspecting the *schedules* given by his Masters that the candidate had completed the necessary residence and attended Lectures in the prescribed subjects, and secondly to examine him in the contents of his books. If he passed this Examination, he was admitted to determine.

Determination was a great day in the student's University life. It retained much of its primitive character of a student's festivity. It was not, it would seem, till the middle of the fifteenth century that the student's Master was required to be officially present at it. The Speech-day of a Public School if combined with considerably more than the licence of the Oxford Encænia or degree day here in May week would perhaps be the nearest modern equivalent of these mediæval exhibitions of rising talent. Every effort was made to attract to the Schools as large an audience as possible, not merely of Masters or fellow-students, but if possible of ecclesiastical dignitaries and other distinguished persons. The friends of a Determiner who was not successful in drawing a more distinguished audience, would run out into the streets and forcibly drag chance passers-by into the School. Wine was provided at the Determiner's expense in the Schools: and the day ended in a feast [given in imitation of the Master's Inception-banquets], even if dancing or torch-light processions were forborne in deference to authority.

I may add here in parenthesis that the thirstiness, always so remarkable in the mediæval man whether it make him strange to you or help to ingratiate him as a human brother, seems to have followed him even into the Tripos. "It was not only after a university exercise," says the historian (Rashdall, vol. ii., p. 687) "but during its progress that the need of refreshment was apt to be felt. . . . Many Statutes allude—some by way of prohibition, but not always—to the custom of providing wine for the Examiners or Temptator [good word] before, during, or after the Examination. At Heidelberg the Dean of the Faculty might order in drinks, the candidate not. At Leipsic the candidate is forbidden to treat [*facere propinam*] the Examiners *before* the Examination: which seems sound. At Vienna (medical school) he is required to spend a florin '*pro confectionibus.*'"

V

Now when we come to England—that is, to Oxford and Cambridge, which ever had queer ways of their own—we find, strange to say, for centuries no evidence at all of any kind of examination. As for *competitive* examinations like the defunct Mathematical and Classical Triposes here—with Senior Wranglers, Wooden Spoons, and what lay between—of all European universities, Louvain alone used the system and may have invented it. At Louvain the candidates for the mastership were placed in three classes, in each of which the names were arranged in order of merit. The first class were styled *Rigorosi* (Honour-men), the second *Transibiles* (Pass-men), the third *Gratiosi* (Charity-passes); while a fourth class, not publicly announced, contained the names of those who could not be passed on any terms. "*Si autem* (*quod absit!*)," says the Statute, "*aliqui inveniantur refutabiles, erunt de quarto ordine.*" "These competitive examinations"—I proceed in the historian's words—"contributed largely to raise Louvain to the high position as a place of learning and education which it retained before the universities were roused from their fifteenth century torpor by the revival of Learning." Pope Adrian VI was one of its famous *Primuses*, and Jansen another. The college which produced a *Primus* enjoyed three days' holiday, during which its bell was rung continuously day and night.

At Oxford and Cambridge (I repeat) we find in their early days no trace of any examination at all. To be sure—and as perhaps you know—the first archives of this University were burned in the "Town and Gown" riots of 1381 by the Townsmen, whose descendants Erasmus describes genially as "combining the utmost rusticity with the utmost malevolence." But no student will doubt that Cambridge used pretty much the same system as Oxford, and the system was this:— When a candidate presented himself before the Chancellor for a Licence in Arts, he had to swear that he had heard certain books,[1] and nine Regent Masters (besides his own Master, who presented him) were required to depose to their knowledge (*de scientia*) of his suffi-

---

[1] Why had he to swear this under pain of excommunication, when the lecturer could so easily keep a roll-call? But the amount of oath taking in a mediæval university was prodigious. Even college servants were put on oath for their duties: Gyps invited their own damnation, bedmakers kissed the book. Abroad, where examinations were held, the Examiner swore not to take a bribe, the Candidate neither to give one, nor, if unsuccessful, to take his vengeance on the Examiner with a knife or other sharp instrument. At New College, Oxford, the matriculating undergraduate was required to swear in particular not to dance in the College Chapel.

ciency: and five others to their credence (*de credulitate*), says the Statute.   Only in the School of Theology was no room allowed to credulity: there all the Masters had to depose "of their knowledge," and one black ball excluded.

VI

Well, you may urge that this method has a good deal to be said for it.   I will go some way to meet you too: but first you must pay me the compliment of supposing me a just man.   Being a just man, and there also being presumed in me some acquaintance with English Literature—not indeed much—not necessarily much— but enough to distinguish good writing from bad or, at any rate, real writing from sham, and at least to have an inkling of what these poets and prose-writers were trying to do—why then I declare to you that, after two years' reading with a man and talk with him about literature, I should have a far better sense of his industry, of his capacity, of his performance and (better) of his promise, than any examination is likely to yield me.   In short I could sign him up for a first, second, or third class, or as *refutabilis*, with more accuracy and confidence than I could derive from taking him as a stranger and pondering his three or four days' performance in a Tripos.   For some of the best men mature slowly: and some, if not most, of the best writers write slowly because they have a conscience; and the most original minds are just those for whom, in a *literary* examination, it is hardest to set a paper.

But the process (you will admit) might be invidious, might lend itself to misunderstanding, might conceivably even lead to re-imposition of an oath forbidding the use of a knife or other sharp implement. And among colleges rivalry is not altogether unknown; and dons, if unlike other men in outward aspect, sometimes resemble them in frailty; and in short I am afraid we shall have to stick to the old system for a while longer. I am sorry, Gentlemen: but you see how it works.

VII

Yet—and I admit it—the main objection abides: that, while Literature deals with *What Is* rather than with *What Knows*, Examinations by their very nature test mere Knowledge rather than anything else: that in the hands of a second-rate examiner they tend to test knowledge alone, or what passes for knowledge: and that in the very run of this world most examiners will be second-rate men: which, if we remind ourselves that they receive the pay of fifth rate ones is, after all, considerably better than we have a right to expect.

We are dealing, mind you, with *English* Literature —our own literature. In examining upon a foreign literature we can artfully lay our stress upon knowledge and yet neither raise nor risk raising the fatal questions, "What is it all *about?*" "What is it, and why is it *it?*" —since merely to translate literally a chorus of the —Agamemnon, or an ode of Pindar's, or a passage from

On Reading for Examinations

Dante or Molière is a creditable performance; to translate either well is a considerable feat; and to translate
either perfectly is what you can't do, and the examiner
knows you can't do, and you know the examiner can't
do, and the examiner knows you know he can't do.   But
when we come to a fine thing in our own language—
to a stanza from Shelley's *Adonais* for instance:

> He has outsoared the shadow of our night;
>   Envy and calumny and hate and pain,
> And that unrest which men miscall delight,
>   Can touch him not and torture not again;
>   From the contagion of the world's slow stain
> He is secure, and now can never mourn
>   A heart grown cold, a head grown grey in vain;
> Nor, when the spirit's self has ceased to burn,
> With sparkless ashes load an unlamented urn—

what can you do with *that?*   How can you examine on
that?   Well, yes, you can request the candidate, to
"Write a short note on the word *calumny* above," or
ask "From what is it derived?"   "What does he know
of *Blackwood's Magazine?*"   "Can he quote any parallel
allusion in Byron?"   You can ask all that: but you are
not getting within measurable distance of *it*.   Your
mind is not even moving on the right plane.   Or let me
turn back to some light and artless Elizabethan thing—
say to the Oenone duet in Peele's *Arraignment of Paris*:

> *Oenone.*   Fair and fair and twice so fair,
>   As fair as any may be:
>   The fairest shepherd on our green,
>   A love for any lady.

Paris.　Fair and fair and twice so fair,
　　　　　　As fair as any may be:
　　　　Thy love is fair for thee alone,
　　　　　　And for no other lady.
Oenone.　My love is fair, my love is gay,
　　　　　　As fresh as bin the flowers in May,
　　　　And of my love my roundelay,
　　　　My merry merry merry roundelay
　　　　　　Concludes with Cupid's curse:
　　　　They that do change old love for new,
　　　　　　Pray gods they change for worse. . . .

　　　　My love can pipe, my love can sing,
　　　　My love can many a pretty thing,
　　　　And of his lovely praises ring
　　　　My merry merry merry roundelays:
　　　　　　"*Amen*" to Cupid's curse:
　　　　They that do change old love for new,
　　　　　　Pray gods they change for worse.
Ambo.　Fair and fair and twice so fair,
　　　　　　As fair as any may be:
　　　　The fairest shepherd on our green,
　　　　　　A love for any lady. . . .

How can anyone examine on *that?* How can any one
solemnly explain, in a hurry, answering one of five or
six questions selected from a three hours' paper, just
why and how that hits him? And yet, if it hit him not,
he is lost. If even so simple a thing as that—a thing of
silly sooth—do not hit him, he is all unfit to traffic with
literature.

VIII

You see how delicate a business it is. Examination
in Literature, being by its very nature so closely tied

down to be a test of *Knowledge*, can hardly, save when used by genius, with care, be any final test of that which is better than Knowledge, of that which is the crown of all scholarship, of *understanding*.

But do not therefore lose heart, even in your reading for strict purposes of examination. Our talk is of reading. Let me fetch you some comfort from the sister and correlative, but harder, art of writing.

I most potently believe that the very best writing, in verse or in prose, can only be produced in moments of high excitement, or rather (as I should put it) in those moments of still and solemn awe into which a noble excitement lifts a man. Let me speak only of prose, of which you may more cautiously allow this than of verse. I think of St. Paul's glorious passage, as rendered in the Authorised version, concluding the fifteenth chapter of his First Epistle to the Corinthians. First, as you know, comes the long, swaying, scholastic, somewhat sophisticated argument about the evidence of resurrection; about the corn, "that which thou sowest," the vivification, the change in vivification, and the rest. All this, almost purely argumentative, should be read quietly, with none of the *bravura* which your prize reader lavishes on it. The argument works up quietly—at once tensely and sinuously, but very quietly—to conviction. Then comes the hush; and then the authoritative voice speaking out of it, awful and slow, "Behold, I shew you a mystery" . . . and then, all the latent emotion of faith taking hold and lifting the man on its surge, "For the trumpet shall sound, and the dead shall be raised incorruptible" . . . and so, incorruption tolling down corruption, the trumpet smashes death underfoot in victory: until out of the midst of tumult, sounds the recall; sober, measured, claiming the purified heart back to discipline. "Therefore, my beloved brethren, be ye stedfast, unmoveable, always abounding in the work of the Lord, forasmuch as ye know that your labour is not in vain in the Lord."

I think of that triumphant passage. I think of the sentences with which Isaak Walton ends his life of Donne. I think of the last pages of Motley's *Dutch Republic*, with its eulogy on William the Silent so exquisitely closing:

As long as he lived, he was the guiding-star of a whole brave nation, and when he died the little children cried in the streets.

I think of two great prose passages in Thackeray's *Esmond;* of Landor's *Dream of Boccaccio* . . . and so on: and I am sure that, in prose or in verse, the best that man can utter flows from him either in moments of high mental excitement or in the hush of that *Altitudo* to which high excitement lifts him.

But, first now, observe how all these passages—and they are the first I call to mind—rise like crests on a large bulk of a wave—St. Paul's on a labouring argument about immortality; Motley's at the conclusion of a heavy task. Long campaigning brings the reward of Harry Esmond's return to Castlewood, long intrigue of the author's mind with his characters closes that

febrile chapter in which Harry walks home to break
the news of the death of the Duke of Hamilton—in
the early morning through Kensington, where the news-
boys are already shouting it:

> The world was going to its business again, although dukes
> lay dead and ladies mourned for them. . . . So day and
> night pass away, and to-morrow comes, and our place knows
> us not. Esmond thought of the courier now galloping on
> the north road to inform him, who was Earl of Arran
> yesterday, that he was Duke of Hamilton to-day, and of a
> thousand great schemes, hopes, ambitions, that were alive
> in the gallant heart, beating but a few hours since, and now
> in a little dust quiescent.

And on top of this let me assure you that in writing, or
learning to write, solid daily practice is the prescription
and "waiting upon inspiration" a lure. These crests
only rise on the back of constant labour. Nine days,
according to Homer, Leto travailed with Apollo: but
he was Apollo, lord of Song. I *know* this to be true of
ordinary talent: but, supposing you all to be geniuses,
I am almost as sure that it holds of genius. Listen to
this:

> Napoleon I used to say that battles were won by the
> sudden flashing of an idea through the brain of a commander
> at a certain critical instant. The capacity for generating
> this sudden electric spark was military genius. . . . Napo-
> leon seems always to have counted upon it, always to have
> believed that when the critical moment arrived the wild
> confusion of the battlefield would be illuminated for him
> by that burst of sudden flame. But if Napoleon had been
> ignorant of the prosaic business of his profession, *to which he*

attended more closely than any other commander, would these moments of supreme clearness have availed him, or would they have come to him at all?

My author thinks not: and I am sure he is right. So, in writing, only out of long preparation can come the truly triumphant flash: and I ask you to push this analogy further, into the business of reading, even of reading for examination. You learn to discipline yourselves, you acquire the art of marshalling, of concentrating, driving your knowledge upon a point: and—for you are young—that point is by no means the final point. Say that it is only an examination, and silly at that. Still you have been learning the art, you have been training yourself to be, for a better purpose, effective.

IX

Yet, and when this has been granted, the crucial question abides and I must not shirk it—"you say that the highest literature deals with *What Is* rather than with *What Knows*. It is all very fine to assure us that testing our knowledge *about* Literature and *around* Literature, and on this side or that side of Literature, is healthy for us in some oblique way: but can you examiners examine, or can you not, on Literature in what you call its own and proper category of *What Is?*"

So I hear the question—the question which beats and has beaten, over and over again, good men trying to construct Schools of English in our universities.

With all sense of a responsibility, of a difficulty, that has lain on my mind for these five years, I answer, Gentlemen, "Yes, we ought: yes, we can: and yes, we will."

But, for the achievement, we teachers must first know how to teach. When that is learned, examination will come as a consequent, easy, almost trivial matter. I will, for example—having already allowed how *hard* it is to examine on literature—take the difficulty at its very extreme. I will select a piece of poetry, and the poet shall be Keats—on whom, if on any one, is felt the temptation to write gush and loose æsthetic chatter. A pupil comes to read with me, and I open at the famous *Ode to a Grecian Urn*.

(1) We read it through together, perhaps twice; at the second attempt getting the emphasis right, and some, at any rate, of the modulations of voice. So we reach a working idea of the Ode and what Keats meant it to be.

(2) We then compare it with his other Odes, and observe that it is (*a*) regular in stanza form, (*b*) in spite of its outburst in the third stanza—"More happy love! more happy, happy love" etc.—much severer in tone than, *e.g.*, the *Ode to a Nightingale* or the *Ode to Psyche*, (*c*) that the emotion is not luscious, but simple, (*d*) that this simplicity is Hellenic, so far as Keats can compass it, and (*e*) eminently well-suited to its subject, which is a carven urn, gracious but severe of outline; a moment of joy caught by the sculptor and arrested, for time to perpetuate; yet—and this is the point of the Ode

—conveying a sense that innocent gaiety is not only its own excuse, but of human things one of the few eternal—and eternal just because it is joyous and fleeting.

(3) Then we go back and compare this kind of quiet immortal beauty with the passionate immortality hymned in the *Nightingale Ode*

> Thou wast not born for death, immortal Bird!
> No hungry generations tread thee down. . .

with all the rest of that supreme stanza: from which (with some passages my reading supplies to illustrate the difference) we fall to contrasting the vibrating thrill of the *Nightingale* with the happy grace of the *Grecian Urn* and, allowing each to be appropriate, dispute for a while, perhaps, over the merits of classical calm and romantic thrill.

(4) From this we proceed to examine the Ode in detail line by line: which examination brings up a whole crowd of questions, such as

(*α*) We have a thought enounced in the first stanza. Does the Ode go on to develop and amplify it, as an Ode should? Or does Pegasus come down again and again on the prints from which he took off? If he do this, and the action of the Ode be dead and unprogressive, is the defect covered by beauty of language? Can such defect ever be so covered?

(*β*) Lines 15 and 16 anticipate lines 21–24, which are saying the same thing and getting no forwarder.

(*γ*) We come to the lines

What little town by river or sea shore
Or mountain-built with peaceful citadel,
Is emptied of this folk, this pious morn?

with the answering lines

And, little town, thy streets for evermore
Will silent be; and not a soul to tell
Why thou art desolate, can e'er return—

and we note Sir Sidney Colvin's suggestion that this breaks in upon an arrest of art as though it were an arrest on reality: and remember that he raised a somewhat similar question over *The Nightingale;* and comparing them, discuss truth of emotion against truth of reality.

We come to the last stanza and lament, "O Attic shape! Fair attitude" for its jingle: but note how the poet recovers himself and brings the whole to a grand close.

I have, even yet, mentioned but a few of the points. For one, I have omitted its most beautiful vowel-play, on which teacher and pupil can dwell and learn together. And heaven forbid that as a teacher I should *insist* even on half of those I have indicated. A teacher, as I hold, should watch for what his pupil divines of his own accord; but if, trafficking with works of inspiration, he have no gift to catch that inspiration nor power to pass it on, then I say, "Heaven help him! but he has no valid right on earth to be in the business."

And if a teacher have all these chances of teaching—mind you, of *accurate* teaching—supplied him by a

7

single Ode of Keats, do you suppose we cannot set in an Examination paper one intelligent question upon it, in its own lawful category?

Gentlemen, with the most scrupulous tenderness for aged and even decrepit interests, we have been trying to liberate you from certain old bad superstitions and silently laying the stones of a new School of English, which we believe to be worthy even of Cambridge.

Our proposals are before the University. Should they be passed, still everything will depend on the loyalty of its teachers to the idea; and on that enthusiasm which I suppose to be the nurse of all studies and know to be the authentic cherishing nurse of ours. We may even have conceded too much to the letter, but we have built and built our trust on the spirit "which maketh alive."

ON A SCHOOL OF ENGLISH

I

IT is now, Gentlemen, five years less a term since, feeling (as they say of other offenders) my position acutely, I had the honour of reading an Inaugural before this University and the impudence to loose, in the course of it, a light shaft against a phrase in the very Ordinance defining the duties of this Chair.

"It shall be the duty of the Professor," says the Ordinance, "to deliver courses of lectures on English Literature from the age of Chaucer onwards, and otherwise to promote, so far as may be in his power, the study in the University of the subject of English Literature."

That was the phrase at which I glanced—"the subject of English Literature"; and I propose that we start to-day, for reasons that will appear, by subjecting this subject to some examination.

II

"The *Subject* of English Literature." Surely—for a start—there is no such thing; or rather, may we not say that everything is, has been or can be, a subject of English Literature? Man's loss of Paradise has been

a subject of English Literature, and so has been a
Copper Coinage in Ireland, and so has been Roast
Sucking-pig, and so has been Holy Dying, and so has
been Mr. Pepys's somewhat unholy living, and so have
been Ecclesiastical Polity, The Grail, Angling for Chub,
the Wealth of Nations, The Sublime and the Beautiful,
The Decline and Fall of the Roman Empire, Prize-
Fights, Grecian Urns, Modern Painters, Intimations of
Immortality in early Childhood, Travels with a Donkey,
Rural Rides and Rejected Addresses—*all* these have
been subjects of English Literature: as have been human
complots and intrigues as wide asunder as *Othello* and
The School for Scandal; persons as different as Prome-
theus and Dr. Johnson, Imogen and Moll Flanders,
Piers the Plowman and Mr. Pickwick; places as differ-
ent as Utopia and Cranford, Laputa and Reading Gaol.
Epipsychidion is literature: but so is *A Tale of a
Tub.*

Listen, for this is literature:

If some king of the earth have so large an extent of do-
minion, in north, and south, so that he hath winter and
summer together in his dominions, so large an extent east
and west as that he hath day and night together in his
dominions much more hath God mercy and judgment together: He brought light out of darkness, not out of a lesser
light; he can bring thy summer out of winter, though thou
have no spring; though in the ways of fortune, or understanding, or conscience, thou have been benighted till now,
wintered and frozen, clouded and eclipsed, damped and be-
numbed, smothered and stupefied till now, now God comes
to thee, not as in the dawning of the day, not as in the bud
of the spring, but as the sun at noon to illustrate all shadows,

as the sheaves in harvest, to fill all penuries, all occasions invite his mercies, and all times are his seasons.[1]

But listen again, for this also is literature:

> A sweet disorder in the dress
> Kindles in clothes a wantonness:
> A lawn about the shoulders thrown
> Into a fine distraction:
> An erring lace, which here and there
> Enthrals the crimson stomacher:
> A cuff neglectful, and thereby
> Ribbons to flow confusedly:
> A winning wave, deserving note,
> In the tempestuous petticoat:
> A careless shoe-string, in whose tie
> I see a wild civility!
> Do more bewitch me than when art
> Is too precise in every part.

Here again is literature:

When I was a child, at seven years old, my friends on a holiday filled my pockets with coppers. I went directly to a shop where they sold toys for children; and being charmed with the sound of a whistle that I met by the way in the hands of another boy, I voluntarily offered him all my money for one. I then came home and went whistling all over the house, much pleased with my whistle but disturbing all the family. My brothers and sisters and cousins, understanding the bargain I had made, told me I had given four times as much for it as it was worth. . . . The reflection gave me more chagrin than the whistle gave me pleasure.

[BENJAMIN FRANKLIN.]

[1] Donne's *Sermon II preached at Pauls upon Christmas Day in the Evening.* 1624.

Of a bridal, this is literature:

> Open the temple gates unto my love,
> Open them wide that she may enter in!

But so also is Suckling's account of a wedding that begins

> I tell thee, Dick, where I have been.

This is literature:

> And a man shall be as an hiding place from the wind, and
> a covert from the tempest;
> As rivers of water in a dry place,
> As the shadow of a great rock in a weary land.

But so is this literature:

> One circle cannot touch another circle on the outside at
> more points than one.
>   For, if it be possible, let the circle ACK touch the circle
> ABC at the points AC.   Join AC.
>   Then because the two points AC are in the circumference
> of the circle ACK the line which joins them falls *within* that
> circle.
>   But the circle ACK is without the circle ABC.   There-
> fore the straight line AC is without the circle ABC.
>   But because the two points A, C are in the circumference
> of ABC therefore the straight line, A, C falls within that
> circle.   *Which is absurd.*
>   Therefore one circle cannot touch another on the outside
> at more points than one.

All thoughts, as well as all passions, all delights

> *votum, timor, ira, voluptas—*

whatsoever, in short, engages man's activity of soul or
body, may be deemed the subject of literature and is

transformed into literature by process of recording it in memorable speech. It is so, it has been so, and God forbid it should ever not be so!

III

Now this, put so, is (you will say) so extremely obvious that it must needs hide a fallacy or at best a quibble on a word. I shall try to show that it does not: that it directly opposes plain truth to a convention accepted by the Ordinance, and that the fallacy lies in that convention.

A convention may be defined as something which a number of men have agreed to accept in lieu of the truth and to pass off for the truth upon others: I was about to add, preferably when they can catch them young: but some recent travel in railway trains and listening to the kind of stuff men of mature years deliver straight out of newspapers for the products of their own digested thought have persuaded me that the ordinary man is as susceptible at fifty, sixty, or even seventy as at any earlier period of growth, and that the process of incubation is scarcely less rapid.

I am not, to be sure, concerned to deny that there may be conventions useful enough to society, serving it to maintain government, order, public and private decency, or the commerce on which it must needs rest to be a civilised society at all—commerce of food, commerce of clothing, and so on, up to commerce in knowledge and ideas. Government itself—any form of it—

is a convention; marriage is a convention; money of
course is a convention, and the alphabet itself I suppose
to contain as many conventions as all the old Courts of
Love and Laws of Chivalry put together, and our
English alphabet one tremendous fallacy, that twenty-
six letters, separately or in combination are capable of
symbolising all the sounds produced by an Englishman's organs of speech, let alone the sounds he hears
from foreigners, dogs, guns, steam-engines, motor-horns
and other friends and enemies to whom we deny the
franchise. Also of course it ignores the whole system of
musical notes—another convention—which yet with
many of the older bards could hardly be separated from
the words they used, though now only the words survive and as literature.

IV

But every convention has a fallacy somewhere at the
root; whether it be useful and operative, as many a legal
fiction is operative, for good; or senile, past service yet
tyrannous by custom, and so pernicious; or merely
foolish, as certain artistic conventions are traceable,
when a Ruskin comes to judgment, back to nothing
better than folly: and it becomes men of honest mind,
in dealing with anything recognisable as a convention,
to examine its accepted fallacy, whether it be well
understood or ill understood; beneficent or pernicious
or merely foolish or both foolish and pernicious: and
this is often most handily done by tracing its history.

Now I shall assume that the framers of the Ordinance regulating the duties of this chair knew well enough, of their own reading, that English Literature deals with a vast variety of subjects: and that, if any piece of writing miss to deal with its particular subject, so closely that theme and treatment can scarcely be separated, by so much will it be faulty as literature. Milton is fairly possessed with the story of Man's fall, Boswell possessed with Johnson, Shelley with hatred of tyranny in all its manifestations, Mill again with the idea of Liberty: and it is only because we had knowledge presented to us at an age when we thought more attentively of apples, that we still fail to recognise in Euclid and Dr. Todhunter two writers who are excellent because possessed with a passion for Geometry.

I infer, then, that the framers of the Ordinance, when they employed this phrase "the study of the subject of English Literature," knew well enough that no such thing existed in nature, but adopted the convention that English Literature could be separated somehow from its content and treated as a subject all by itself, for teaching purposes: and, for purposes of examination, could be yoked up with another subject called English Language, as other universities had yoked it.

V

I believe the following to be a fair account of how these examinations in English Language and Literature came to pass, and how a certain kind of student came to pass these Examinations. At any rate since the small revolution has happened in my life-time and most of it since I was able to observe, the account here is drawn from my own observation and may be checked and corrected by yours.

Thirty-five or forty years ago—say in the late seventies or early eighties—some preparatory schools, and others that taught older boys but ranked below the great Public Schools in repute, taught so much of English Literature as might be comprised, at a rough calculation, in two or three plays of Shakespeare, edited by Clark and Aldis Wright; a few of Bacon's Essays, Milton's early poems, Stopford Brooke's little primer, a book of extracts for committal to memory, with perhaps Chaucer's *Prologue* and a Speech of Burke. In the great Public Schools *no* English Literature was studied, save in those which had invented "Modern Sides," to prepare boys specially for Woolwich or Sandhurst or the Indian Civil Service; for entrance to which examinations were held on certain prescribed English Classics, and marks mainly given for acquaintance with the editors' notes.

In the universities, the study of English Classics was not officially recognised at all.

Let us not hastily suppose that this neglect of English rested wholly on unreason, or had nothing to say for itself. Teachers and tutors of the old Classical Education (as it was called) could plead as follows:

"In the first place," they would say, "English Literature is too *easy* a study. Our youth, at school or university,

starts on his native classics with a hability which in any
foreign language he has painfully to acquire. The voices
that murmured around his cradle, the voice of his nurse, of
his governess, of the parson on Sundays; the voices of village
boys, stablemen, gamekeepers, and farmers—friendly or
unfriendly—of callers, acquaintances, of the children he
met at Children's Parties; the voices that at the dinner-
table poured politics or local gossip into the little pitcher
with long ears—all these were English voices speaking in
English: and all these were all the while insensibly leading
him up the slope from the summit of which he can survey
the promised land spread at his feet as a wide park; and he
holds the key of the gates, to enter and take possession.
Whereas," the old instructors would continue, "with the
classics of any foreign language we take him at the foot of
the steep ascent, spread a table before him (*mensa, mensa,
mensam* . . . and coax or drive him up with variations
upon *amo*, 'I love' or πίπτω, 'I beat,' until he, too, reaches
the summit and beholds the landscape:

> But O, what labour!
> O Prince, what pain!"

Now so much of truth, Gentlemen, as this plea contains was admitted last term by your Senate, in sepa-
rating the English Tripos, in which a certain linguistic
familiarity may be not rashly presumed of the student,
from the Foreign Language Triposes, divided into two
parts, of which the first will more suspiciously test his
capacity to construe the books he professes to have
studied. I may return to this and to the alleged *easiness*
of studies in a School of English. Let us proceed just
now with the reasoned plea for neglect.

These admirable old schoolmasters and dons would
have hesitated, maybe, to say flatly with Dogberry that

"to write and read comes by nature . . . and for your writing and reading, let that appear when there is no need of such vanity." But in practice their system so worked, and in some of the Public Schools so works to this day. Let me tell you that just before the war an undergraduate came to me from the Sixth Form of one of the best reputed among these great schools. He wished to learn to write. He wished (poor fellow) to write me an essay, if I would set him a subject. He had never written an essay at school. "Indeed," said I, "and there is no reason why you should, if by 'essay' you mean some little treatise about 'Patriotism' or 'A Day in the Country.' I will choose you no such subject nor any other upon any book which you have never read. Tell me, what is your Tripos?" He said "the History Tripos." "Then," said I, "since History provides quite a large number of themes, choose one and I will try to correct your treatment of it, without offence to your opinions or prejudice to your facts." "But," he confessed, "at So-and-so"—naming the great Public School—"we never *wrote* out an account of anything, or set down our opinions on anything, to be corrected. We just construed and did sums." And when he brought me his first attempt, behold, it was so. He could not construct a simple sentence, let alone putting two sentences together; while, as for a paragraph, it lay beyond his farthest horizon. In short, here was an instance ready to hand for any cheap writer engaged to decry the old Classical Education.

What would the old schoolmasters plead in excuse?

Why this, as I suggest—"You cite an extreme instance. But, while granting English Literature to be great, we would point out that an overwhelming majority of our best writers have modelled their prose and verse upon the Greek and Roman classics, either directly or through tradition. Now we have our own language *gratis*, so to speak. Let us spend our pains, then, in acquiring Latin and Greek, and the tradition. So shall we most intimately enjoy our own authors; and so, if we wish to write, we shall have at hand the clues they followed, the models they used."

Now I have, as you know, Gentlemen, a certain sympathy with this plea, or with a part of it: nor can so much of truth as its argument contains be silenced by a "What about Shakespeare?" or a "What about Bunyan?" or a "What about Burns?" I believe our imaginary pleader for the Classics could put up a stout defence upon any of those names. To choose the forlornest hope of the three, I can hear him demonstrating, to his own satisfaction if not to yours, that Bunyan took his style straight out of the Authorised Version of our Bible; which is to say that he took it from the styles of forty-seven scholars, *plus* Tyndale's, *plus* Coverdale's, *plus* Cranmer's—the scholarship of fifty scholars expressed and blended.

But, as a theory, the strict classical argument gives itself away, as well by its intolerance as by its obvious distrust of the genius of our own wonderful language. I have in these five years, and from this place, Gentlemen, counselled you to seek back ever to those

Mediterranean sources which are the well-heads of our civilisation: but always (I hope) on the understanding that you use them with a large liberty. They are effete for us unless we add and mingle freely the juice of our own natural *genius*.

And in practice the strict classical theory, with its implied contempt of English, has been disastrous: disastrous not only with the ordinary man—as with my Sixth Form boy who could not put two sentences together, and had read no English authors; but disastrous even to highly eminent scholars. Listen, pray, to this passage from one of them, Frederick Paley, who condescended (Heaven knows why) to turn the majestic verse of Pindar into English Prose—

From the VIIIth Isthmian:

And now that we are returned from great sorrows, let us not fall into a dearth of victories, nor foster griefs; but as we have ceased from our tiresome troubles, we will publicly indulge in a sweet roundelay.

From the IVth Pythian:

It had been divinely predicted to Pelias, that he should die by the doughty sons of Æolus . . . and an alarming oracle had come to his wary mind, delivered at the central point of tree-clad mother-earth, "that he must by all means hold in great caution the man with one shoe, when he shall have come from a homestead on the hills."

And he accordingly came in due time, armed with two spears, a magnificent man. The dress he wore was of a double kind, the material costume of the Magnesians. . . . Nor as yet had the glossy clusters of his hair been clipped away, but dangled brightly adown his back.

Forward he went at once and took his stand among the people. . . . Him then they failed to recognise: but some of the reverent-minded went so far as to say, "Surely this cannot be Apollo!"

It needs no comment, I think. Surely *this* cannot be Apollo!

Frederick Paley flourished—if the word be not exorbitant for so demure a writer—in the middle of the last century (he was born in the year of Waterloo and died in the year after Queen Victoria's first Jubilee). Well, in that period there grew up a race of pioneers who saw that English Literature—that proud park and rolling estate—lay a tangled, neglected wilderness for its inheritors, and set themselves bravely to clear broad ways through it. Furnivall and Skeat, Aldis Wright, Clark, Grosart, Arber, Earle, Hales, Morris, Ellis, and the rest—who can rehearse these names now but in deepest respect? Oh, believe me, Gentlemen! they were wonderful fighters in a cause that at first seemed hopeless. If I presume to speak of foibles to-day, you will understand that I do so because, lightly though I may talk to you at times, I have a real sense of the responsibilities of this Chair. I worship great learning, which they had: I loathe flippant detraction of what is great; I have usually a heart for men-against-odds and the unpopular cause. But these very valiant fighters had, one and all, some very obvious foibles: and because, in the hour of success, these foibles came to infect the whole teaching of English in this country, and to infect it fatally for many years, I shall dare to point them out.

VI

(*a*) To begin with, then, these valiant fighters, intent on pushing their cause to the front, kept no sense of proportion. All their geese were swans, and *Beowulf* a second *Iliad*. I think it scarcely too much to say that, of these men, all so staunch in fighting for the claims of English Literature, not one (with the exception of Dr. Hales) appears to have had any critical judgment whatever, apart from the rhyme, verse, and inflectional tests on which they bestowed their truly priceless industry. Criticism, as Sainte Beuve, Matthew Arnold, or Pater understood and practised it, they merely misprized.

(*b*) I think it was of true scholarly desire to vindicate English Literature from the charge of being "too easy," that—as their studies advanced—they laid more and more stress on Middle-English and Old English writings than on what our nations of England and Scotland have written since they learned to write. I dare to think also that we may attribute to this dread of "easiness" their practice of cumbering simple texts with philological notes; on which, rather than on the text, we unhappy students were carefully examined. For an example supplied to Dr. Corson—I take those three lines of Cowper's *Task* (Bk. I, 86–88):

> Thus first necessity invented stools,
> Convenience next suggested elbow-chairs,
> And luxury th' accomplish'd SOFA last.

Now in these three lines the word "*accomplish'd*" is the only one that needs even the smallest explanation.

"But," says Dr. Corson, "in two different editions of *The Task* in my library, prepared for the use of the young, no explanation is given of it, but in both the Arabic origin of "sofa" is given. In one the question is asked what other words in English have been derived from the Arabic." ("Abracadabra" would be my little contribution.)

(*c*) These valiant fighters—having to extol what Europe had, wrongly enough, forgotten to count among valuable things—turned aggressively provincial, parted their beards in the Anglo-Saxon fashion; composed long sentences painfully innocent of any word not derivable from Anglo-Saxon, sentences in which the "impenetrability of matter" became the "un-go-throughsomeness of stuff" (but that may have happened in a parody), and in general comported themselves like the Anglo-Saxons they claimed for their forbears; rightly enough for anything any one cared, but wrongly enough for the rest of us who had no yearning toward that kinship and went on spelling Alfred with an A.

(*d*) They were—I suppose through opposition—extremely irascible men; like farmers. Urbanity was the last note in their gamut, the City—*urbs quam dicunt Roman*—the last of places in their ken. There was no engaging them in dialectic, an Athenian art which they frankly despised. If you happened to disagree with them, their answer was a sturdy Anglo-Saxon brick. If you politely asked your way to Puddlehampton, and to be directed to Puddlehampton's main objects of interest, the answer you would get (see "*Notes and*

8

Queries" passim) would be, "Who is this that comes out of Nowhere, enquiring for Puddlehampton, unacquainted with Stubbs? Is it possible at this time of day that the world can contain any one ignorant of the published Transactions of the Wiltshire Walking Club, vol. iii., p. 159—*Puddlehampton, its Rise and Decline, with a note on Vespasian.*"

(*e*) These pioneers—pushing the importance of English, but occupied more and more with origins and with bad authors, simply could not see the vital truth; that English Literature is a continuing thing, ten times more alive to-day than it was in the times they studied and belauded. The last word upon them is that not a man of them could write prose in the language they thrust on our study. To them, far more than to the old classical scholars, English was a shut book; a large book, but closed and clasped, material to heighten a desk for schoolmasters and schoolmistresses.

But schoolmasters and schoolmistresses, like chickens and curses, come home to roost. Once set up your plea for a Tripos of English Language and Literature on the lower plea that it will provide for what *they* call a "felt want," and sooner or later you give English Language and Literature into *their* hands, and then you get the fallacy full-flowered into a convention. English Literature henceforth is a "subject," divorced from life: and what they have made of it, let a thousand handbooks and so-called histories attest. But this world is not a wilderness of class-rooms. English Language? They cannot write it, at all events. They do not (so

far as I can discover) try to write it.   They talk and write
about it; how the poor deceased thing outgrew infantile
ailments, how it was operated on for *umlaut*, how it
parted with its vermiform appendix and its inflexions
one by one and lost its vowel endings in muted e's.

> And they went and told the sexton,
> And the sexton toll'd the bell.

But when it comes to *writing;* to keeping bright the
noble weapon of English, testing its poise and edge,
feeling the grip, handing it to their pupils with the word,
"Here is the sword of your fathers, that has cloven
dragons.   So use it, that we who have kept it bright
may be proud of you, and of our pains, and of its continuing valiance":—why, as I say, they do not even *try*.
Our unprofessional forefathers, when they put pen to
paper, did attempt English prose, and not seldom
achieved it.   But take up any elaborate History of English Literature and read, and, as you read, ask yourselves, "How can one of the rarest delights of life be
converted into *this?*   What has happened to merry
Chaucer, rare Ben Jonson, gay Steele and Prior, to
Goldsmith, Jane Austen, Charles Lamb?"

> All, all are gone, the old familiar faces!

gone into the professional stock-pot!   And the next
news is that these cooks, of whom Chaucer wrote pro-
phetically,

> These cookes, how they stampe and streyne and grinde,
> And turnen substaunce into accident,

have formed themselves into professional Associations
to protect "the study of the subject of English Literature" and bark off any intruder who would teach in
another way than theirs.

VII

But I say to you that Literature is not, and should
not be, the preserve of any priesthood. To write English, so as to make Literature, may be *hard*. But English Literature is *not* a mystery, *not* a Professors'
Kitchen.

And the trouble lies, not in the harm professionising
does to schoolmasters and schoolmistresses, but in the
harm it does "in widest commonalty spread" among
men and women who, as Literature was written for
them, addressed to them, ought to find in it, all their
lives through, a retirement from mean occupations, a
well of refreshment, sustainment in the daily drudgery
of life, solace in calamity, an inmate by the hearth, ever
sociable, never intrusive—to be sought and found, to be
found and dropped at will:

> Men, when their affairs require
> Must themselves at whiles retire.
> Sometimes hunt, and sometimes hawk
> And not ever sit and talk—

to be dropped at will and left without any answering
growl of moroseness; to be consulted again at will and
found friendly.

For this is the trouble of *professionising* Literature. We exile it from the business of life, in which it would ever be at our shoulder, to befriend us. Listen, for example, to an extract from a letter written, a couple of weeks ago, by somebody in the Charity Commission:

Sir,

With reference to previous correspondence in this matter, I am to say that in all the circumstances of this case the Commissioners are of the opinion that it would be desirable that a public enquiry in connection with the Charity should be held in the locality.

And the man—very likely an educated man—having written *that*, very likely went home and read Chaucer, Dante, or Shakespeare, or Burke for pleasure! That is what happens when you treat literature as a "subject," separable from life and daily practice.

VIII

I declare to you that Literature was *not* written for schoolmasters or for schoolmistresses. I would not exchange it for a wilderness of schoolmasters. It should be delivered from them, who, with their silly *ablauts* and "tendencies," can themselves neither read nor write. For the proof? Having the world's quintessential store of mirth and sharp sorrow, wit, humour, comfort, farce, comedy, tragedy, satire; the glories of our birth and state, piled all at their elbows, only one man of the crowd—and he M. Jusserand, a Frenchman

—has contrived to draw out of the mass one interesting well-written history of the "subject."

IX

Is there, then, no better way? Yes there is a better way: for the French have it, with their language and literature. In France, as Matthew Arnold noted, a generation ago, the ordinary journey-man work of literature is done far better and more conscientiously than with us. In France a man feels it almost a personal stain, an unpatriotic *lâche* to write even on a police-order anything so derogatory to the tradition of his language as our Cabinet Ministers read out as answers to our House of Commons. I am told that many a Maire in a small provincial town in N. E. France, even when overwhelmed—*accablé*—with the sufferings of his town-folk, has truly felt the iron enter into his soul on being forced to sign a document written out for him in the invaders' French.

Cannot we treat our noble inheritance of literature and language as scrupulously, and with as high a sense of their appertaining to our national honour, as a Frenchman cherishes *his* language, *his* literature? Cannot we study to leave our inheritance—as the old Athenian put it temperately, "not worse but a little better than we found it?"

I think we can, and should. I shall close to-day, Gentlemen, with the most modest of perorations. In my first lecture before you, in January, 1913, I quoted to you the artist in *Don Quixote* who, being asked what animal he was painting, answered diffidently, "That is as it may turn out."

The teaching of our language and literature is, after all, a new thing and still experimental. The main tenets of those who, aware of this, have worked on the scheme for a School of English in Cambridge, the scheme recently passed by your Senate and henceforth to be in operation, are three:

The first. That literature cannot be divorced from life: that (for example) you cannot understand Chaucer aright, unless you have the background, unless you know the kind of men for whom Chaucer wrote and the kind of men whom he made speak; that is the *national* side with which all our literature is concerned.

The second. Literature being so personal a thing, you cannot understand it until you have some personal understanding of the men who wrote it. Donne is Donne; Swift, Swift; Pope, Pope; Johnson, Johnson; Goldsmith, Goldsmith; Charles Lamb, Charles Lamb; Carlyle, Carlyle. Until you have grasped those men, as men, you cannot grasp their writings. That is the *personal* side of literary study, and as necessary as the other.

The third. That the writing and speaking of English is a living art, to be practised and (if it may be) improved. That what these great men have done is to hand us a grand patrimony; that they lived to support us through the trial we are now enduring, and to carry us through to great days to come. So shall our sons, now fighting in France, have a language ready for the land they shall recreate and repeople.

THE VALUE OF GREEK AND LATIN
IN ENGLISH LITERATURE

I

I HAVE promised you, Gentlemen, for to-day some
observations on *The Value of Greek and Latin in
English Literature:* a mild, academic title, a *camouflage*
title, so to say; calculated to shelter us for a while from
the vigilance of those hot-eyed reformers who, had I
advertised *The Value of Greek and Latin in English
Life* might even now be swooping from all quarters of
the sky on a suggestion that these dry bones yet were
flesh: for the eyes I dread are not only red and angry,
but naturally microscopic—and that indeed, if they
only knew it, is their malady. Yet "surely," groaned
patient Job, "there *is* a path which the vulture's eye
hath not seen!"

You, at any rate, know by this time that wherever
these lectures assert literature they assert life, perhaps
even too passionately, allowing neither the fact of death
nor the possibility of divorce.

II

But let us begin with the first word, " *Value*"—"The
Value of Greek and Latin in English Literature." What

do I mean by "Value." Well, I use it, generally, in the
sense of "worth"; but with a particular meaning, or
shade of meaning, too. And, this particular meaning
is not the particular meaning intended (as I suppose)
by men of commerce who, on news of a friend's death,
fall a-musing and continue musing until the fire kindles,
and they ask, "What did So-and-so die worth?" or
sometimes, more wisely than they know, "What did
poor old So-and-so die worth?" or again, more collo-
quially, "What did So-and-so 'cut up' for?" Neither
is it that which more disinterested economists used to
teach; men never (I fear me) loved, but anyhow lost
awhile, who for my green-unknowing youth, at Thebes
or Athens—growing older I tend to forget which is,
or was, which—defined the Value of a thing as its "pur-
chasing power," which the market translates into
"price." For—to borrow a phrase which I happened
on, the other day, with delight, in the preface to a
translation of Lucian—there may be forms of education less paying than the commercial and yet better
worth paying for; nay, above payment or computation
in price.[1]

No: the particular meaning I use to-day is that
which artists use when they talk of painting or of
music. To see things, near or far, in their true perspective and proportions; to judge them through distance; and fetching them back, to reproduce them in
art so proportioned comparatively, so rightly adjusted,

---

[1] The Works of Lucian of Samosata: translated by H. W. Fowler and
F. G. Fowler (Introduction, p. xxix). Oxford, Clarendon Press.

that they combine to make a particular and just perspective: that is to give things their true *Values*.

Suppose yourself reclining on a bank on a clear day,
looking up into the sky and watching the ascent of a
skylark while you listen to his song. That is a posture
in which several poets of repute have placed themselves
from time to time: so we need not be ashamed of it.
Well, you see the atmosphere reaching up and up, mile
upon mile. There are no milestones planted there. But
wave on wave perceptible, the atmosphere stretches up
through indeterminate distances; and according as your
painter of the sky can translate these distances, he gives
his sky what is called *Value*.

You listen to the skylark's note rising, spiral by
spiral, on "the very jet of earth":

> As up he wings the spiral stair,
> 　A song of light, and pierces air
> With fountain ardour, fountain play,
> 　To reach the shining tops of day:

and you long for the musical gift to follow up and up
the delicate degrees of distance and thread the notes
back as the bird ascending drops them—on a thread,
as it were, of graduated beads, half music and half
dew:

> That was the chirp of Ariel
> You heard, as overhead it flew,
> The farther going more to dwell
> And wing our green to wed our blue;
> But whether note of joy, or knell,
> Not his own Father-singer knew;

> Nor yet can any mortal tell,
> Save only how it shivers through;
> The breast of us a sounded shell,
> The blood of us a lighted dew.

Well, in music, in painting, this graduating which gives right proportion and, with proportion, a sense of distance, of atmosphere, is called *Value*. Let us, for a minute or two, assay this particular meaning of Value upon life and literature, and first upon life, or, rather upon one not negligible facet of life.

I suppose that if an ordinary man of my age were asked which has better helped him to bear the burs of life—religion or a sense of humour—he would, were he quite honest, be gravelled for an answer. Now the best part of a sense of humour, as you know without my telling you, consists in a sense of proportion; a habit, abiding and prompt at command, of seeing all human affairs in their just perspective, so that its happy possessor at once perceives anything odd or distorted or overblown to be an excrescence, a protuberance, a swelling, literally a *humour:* and the function of Thalia, the Comic Spirit, as you may read in Meredith's *Essay on Comedy*, is just to prick these humours. I will but refer you to Meredith's *Essay*, and here cite you the words of an old schoolmaster:

It would seem to be characteristic of the same mind to appreciate the beauty of ideas in just proportion and harmonious relation to each other, and the absurdity of the same ideas when distorted or brought into incongruous juxtaposition. The exercise of this sense of humour . . .

compels the mind to form a picture to itself, accompanied by pleasurable emotion; and what is this but setting the imagination to work, though in topsy-turvy fashion? Nay, in such a case, imagination plays a double part, since it is only by instantaneous comparison with ideal fitness and proportion that it can grasp at full force the grotesqueness of their contraries.[1]

Let us play with an example for one moment. A child sees such an excrescence, such an offence upon proportion, in an immoderately long nose. He is apt to call attention to it on the visage of a visitor: it intrigues him in Perrault's "Prince Charming" and many a fairy tale: it amuses him in Lear's *Book of Nonsense:*

> There was an old man with a Nose,
> Who said, "If you choose to suppose
> That my nose is too long
> You are certainly wrong—"

This old man, he detects as lacking sense of proportion, sense of humour. Pass from the child to the working-man as we know him. A few weeks ago, a lady featured, as to nose, on the side of excess—was addressing a North Country audience on the Economic Position of Women after the War. Said she, "There won't be men to go round." Said a voice, "Eh, but they'll *have to*, Miss!" Pass from this rudimentary criticism to high talent employed on the same subject, and you get *Cyrano de Bergerac.* Pass to genius, to Milton, and you

---

[1] *The Training of the Imagination:* by James Rhoades. London, John Lane, 1900.

find the elephant amusing Adam and Eve in Paradise, and doing his best:

> the unwieldy elephant,
> To make them mirth, used all his might, and wreathed
> His lithe proboscis.

Milton, like the elephant, jokes with difficulty, but he, too, is using all his might.

III

I have illustrated, crudely enough, how a sense of things in their right values will help us on one side of our dealings with life.   But truly it helps us on every side.   This was what Plato meant when he said that a philosopher must see things as they relatively are within his horizon—ὁ συνοπτικὸς διαλεκτικός.   And for this it was that an English poet praised Sophocles as one

> Who saw life steadily, and saw it whole.

And this of course is what Dean Inge meant when, the other day, in a volume of *Cambridge Essays on Education*, he reminded us, for a sensible commonplace, that "The wise man is he who knows the relative values of things."

IV

Applying this to literature, I note, but shall not insist here on the fact—though fact it is—that the

Greek and Roman "classical" writers (as we call them) laid more stress than has ever been laid among the subsequent tribes of men upon the desirability of getting all things into proportion, of seeing all life on a scale of relative values. And the reason I shall not insist on this is simply that better men have saved me the trouble.

I propose this morning to discuss the value of the classics to students of English literature from, as the modern phrase goes, a slightly different angle.

Reclining and looking up into that sky which is not too grandiose an image for our own English Literature, you would certainly not wish, Gentlemen, to see it as what it is not—as a cloth painted on the flat. No more than you would choose the sky overarching your life to be a close, hard, copper vault, would you choose this literature of ours to resemble such a prison. I say nothing, for the moment, of the thrill of comparing ours with other constellations—of such a thrill as Blanco White's famous sonnet imagines in Adam's soul when the first night descended on Eden and

> Hesperus with the host of heaven came,
> And lo! Creation widen'd in man's view.
> Who could have thought such darkness lay conceal'd
> Within thy beams, O sun! . . .

No: I simply picture you as desiring to realise *our own* literature, *its* depths and values, mile above mile deeper and deeper shining, with perchance a glimpse of a city celestial beyond, or at whiles, on a ladder of values, of the angels—the messengers—climbing and returning.

V

Well, now, I put it to you that without mental breeding, without at least some sense of ancestry, an Englishman can hardly have this perception of value, this vision. I put to you what I posited in an earlier course of lectures, quoting Bagehot, that while a knowledge of Greek and Latin is not necessary to a writer of English, he should at least have a firm conviction that those two languages existed. I refer you to a long passage which, in one of those lectures, I quoted from Cardinal Newman to the effect that for the last three thousand years the Western World has been evolving a human society, having its bond *in a common civilisation*—a society to which (let me add, by way of footnote), Prussia to-day is firmly, though with great difficulty, being tamed. There are, and have been, other civilisations in the world—the Chinese, for instance; a huge civilisation, stationary, morose, to us unattractive; "but *this* civilisation," says Newman, "together with the society which is its creation and its home, is so distinctive and luminous in its character, so imperial in its extent, so imposing in its duration, and so utterly without rival upon the face of the earth, that the association may fitly assume for itself the title of 'Human Society,' and its civilisation the abstract term 'Civilisation.'"

He goes on:

Looking, then, at the countries which surround the Mediterranean Sea as a whole, I see them to be, from time immemorial, the seat of an association of intellect and mind

such as deserves to be called the Intellect and Mind of the
Human Kind.

But I must refer you to his famous book *The Idea
of a University* to read at length how Newman, in
that sinuous, sinewy, Platonic style of his, works it
out—the spread, through Rome, even to our shores,
of the civilisation which began in Palestine and
Greece.

VI

I would press the point more rudely upon you, and
more particularly, than does Newman. And first, for
Latin—

I waive that Rome occupied and dominated this
island during four hundred years. Let that be as though
it had never been. For a further one thousand years
and more Latin remained the common speech of educated men throughout Europe: the "Universal Language." Greek had been smothered by the Turk.
Through all that time—through the most of what we
call Modern History, Latin reigned everywhere. Is
this a fact to be ignored by any of you who would value
"values?"

Here are a few particulars, by way of illustration.
More wrote his *Utopia*, Bacon his *Essays* and all the
bulk of his philosophical work, in Latin; Newton wrote
his *Principia* in Latin. Keble's Lectures on Poetry (if
their worth and the name of Keble may together save
me from bathos) were delivered in Latin. Our Vice-

Chancellor, our Public Orator still talk Latin, securing for it what attention they can: nor have

> The bigots of this iron time
> *Yet* call'd their harmless art a crime.

But there is a better reason why you should endeavour to understand the value of Latin in our literature; a filial reason.   Our fathers built their great English prose, as they built their oratory, upon the Latin model. Donne used it to construct his mighty fugues.   Burke to discipline his luxuriance.   Says Cowper, "It were

> 'Praise enough' for any private man,
> That Chatham's language was his mother tongue,
> And Wolfe's great name compatriot with his own."

Well then, here is a specimen of Chatham's language: from his speech, Romanly severe, denouncing the Government of the day for employing Red Indians in the American War of Independence.   He is addressing the House of Lords:

I call upon that right reverend bench, those holy ministers of the Gospel, and pious pastors of our Church—I conjure them to join in the holy work, and vindicate the religion of their God.   I appeal to the wisdom and the law of this learned bench to defend and support the justice of their country.   I call upon the bishops to interpose the unsullied sanctity of their lawn; upon the learned judges to interpose the purity of their ermine, to save us from this pollution.   I call upon the honour of your lordships to reverence the dignity of your ancestors, and to maintain your own.   I call upon the spirit and humanity of my country to vindicate the national character.   I invoke the genius of the

9

Constitution. From the tapestry that adorns these walls the immortal ancestor of this noble lord [Lord Suffolk] frowns with indignation at the disgrace of his country. In vain he led your victorious fleets against the boasted Armada of Spain; in vain he defended and established the honour, the liberties, the religion—the *Protestant religion*—of this country, against the arbitrary cruelties of Popery and the Inquisition, if these more than Popish cruelties and inquisitorial practices are let loose among us—to turn forth into our settlements, among our ancient connexions, friends, and relations, the merciless cannibal, thirsting for the blood of man, woman, and child! to send forth the infidel savage—against whom? against your Protestant brethren; to lay waste their country, to desolate their dwellings, and extirpate their race and name, with these horrible hell-hounds of savage war!—hell-hounds, I say, of savage war! Spain armed herself with blood-hounds to extirpate the wretched natives of America, and we improve on the inhuman example even of Spanish cruelty; we turn loose these savage hell-hounds against our brethren and countrymen in America, of the same language, laws, liberties, and religion, endeared to us by every tie that should sanctify humanity . . .

My lords, I am old and weak, and at present unable to say more; but my feelings and indignation were too strong to have said less. I could not have slept this night in my bed, nor reposed my head on my pillow, without giving this vent to my eternal abhorrence of such preposterous and enormous principles.

That was Chatham. For Wolfe—he, as you know, was ever reading the classics even on campaign: as Burke again carried always a Virgil in his pocket. *Abeunt studia in mores.* Moreover can we separate Chatham's Roman morality from Chatham's language in the passage I have just read? No: we cannot. No one, being evil can speak good things, with that weight; "*for out*

of the abundance of the heart the mouth speaketh." We
English (says Wordsworth)

> We must be free or die, who speak the tongue
> That Shakespeare spake. . . .

You may criticise Chatham's style as too consciously
Ciceronian. But has ever a Parliamentary style been
invented which conveys a nobler gravity of emotion?
"Buskined?"—yes: but the style of a man. "Man-
nered?"—yes, but in the grand manner. "Conscious?"
—yes, but of what? Conscious of the dignity a great
man owes to himself, and to the assembly he addresses.
He conceives that assembly as "the British Senate";
and, assuming, he communicates that high conception.
The Lords feel that they are listening as Senators, since
it is only thus a Senate should be addressed, as nothing
less than a Senate should be addressed thus.

Let me read you a second passage; of *written* prose:

Laodameia died; Helen died; Leda, the beloved the Jupi-
ter went before. It is better to repose in the earth betimes
than to sit up late; better, than to cling pertinaciously to
what we feel crumbling under us, and to protract an inevitable fall. We may enjoy the present while we are insensible
of infirmity and decay: but the present, like a note in music,
is nothing but as it appertains to what is past and what is
to come. There are no fields of amaranth on this side of the
grave; there are no voices, O Rhodopè! that are not soon
mute, however tuneful; there is no name, with whatever
emphasis of passionate love repeated, of which the echo is
not faint at last.[1]

[1] Landor: *Æsop and Rhodopè.*

Latin—all Latin—down to its exquisite falling close!
And I say to you, Gentlemen, that passages such as
these deserve what Joubert claimed of national monuments, *Ce sont les crampons qui unissent une génération à
une autre.   Conservez ce qu'ont vu vos pères,* "These are
the clamps that knit one generation to another.   Cherish
those things on which your fathers' eyes have looked."
Abeunt studia in mores.

If, years ago, there had lacked anything to sharpen
my suspicion of those fork-bearded professors who derived our prose from the stucco of Anglo-Saxon prose, it
would have been their foolish deliberate practice of
composing whole pages of English prose without using
one word derivative from Latin or Greek.   Esau, when
he sold his birthright, had the excuse of being famished.
These pedants, with a full board, sought frenetically to
give it away—board and birthright.   "*So when this
corruptible shall have put on incorruption, and this mortal
shall have put on immortality*"—almost, I say, these
men had deserved to have a kind of speech more to
their taste read over their coffins.

VII

What, in the next place, can I say of Greek, save
that, as Latin gave our fathers the model of prose,
Greek was the source of it all, the goddess and genius
of the well-head?   And, casting about to illustrate, as
well as may be, what I mean by this, I hit on a minor
dialogue of Plato, the *Phaedrus,* and choose you a short
passage in Edward FitzGerald's rendering:

When Socrates and Phædrus have discourses away the noon-day under the plane trees by the Ilyssus, they rise to depart toward the city. But Socrates (pointing perhaps to some images of Pan and other sylvan deities) says it is not decent to leave their haunts without praying to them, and he prays:

"O auspicious Pan, and ye other deities of this place, grant to me to become beautiful *inwardly*, and that all my outward goods may prosper my inner soul. Grant that I may esteem wisdom the only riches, and that I may have so much gold as temperance can handsomely carry.

"Have we yet aught else to pray for, Phaedrus? For myself I seem to have prayed enough."

Phaedrus: "Pray as much for me also: for friends have all in common."

Socrates: "Even so be it. Let us depart."

To this paternoster of Socrates, reported more than four centuries before Christ taught the Lord's Prayer, let me add an attempted translation of the lines that close Homer's hymn to the Delian Apollo. Imagine the old blind poet on the beach chanting to the islanders the glorious boast of the little island—how it of all lands had harboured Leto in her difficult travail; how she gave birth to the Sun God; how the immortal child, as the attendant goddesses touched his lips with ambrosia, burst his swaddling bands and stood up, sudden, a god erect:

> But he, the Sun-God, did no sooner taste
>   That food divine than every swaddling band
>   Burst strand by strand,
> And burst the belt above his panting waist—
>   All hanging loose
> About him as he stood and gave command:

"Fetch me my lyre, fetch me my curving bow!
    And, taught by these, shall know
All men, through me, the unfaltering will of Zeus!"
So spake the unshorn God, the Archer bold,
    And turn'd to tread the ways of Earth so wide;
While they, all they, had marvel to behold
        How Delos broke in gold
Beneath his feet, as on a mountain-side
Sudden, in Spring, a tree is glorified
    And canopied with blossoms manifold.
But he went swinging with a careless stride,
    Proud, in his new artillery bedight,
Up rocky Cynthus, and the isles descried—
All his, and their inhabitants—for wide,
Wide as he roam'd, ran these in rivalry
To build him temples in many groves:
And these be his, and all the isles he loves,
        And every foreland height,
And every river hurrying to the sea.
        But chief in thee,
Delos, as first it was, is his delight.
Where the long-robed Ionians, each with mate
    And children, pious to his altar throng,
        And, decent, celebrate
His birth with boxing-match and dance and song:
So that a stranger, happening them among,
Would deem that these Ionians have no date,
    Being ageless, all so met;
        And he should gaze
        And marvel at their ways,
    Health, wealth, the comely face
On man and woman—envying their estate—
                    And yet
You can be ne'er able to forget,
You maids of Delos, dear ones, as ye raise
The hymn to Phoebus, Leto, Artemis,
        In triune praise,

Then slide your song back upon ancient days
And men whose very name forgotten is,
And women who have lived and gone their ways:
    And make them live agen,
    Charming the tribes of men,
Whose speech ye mock with pretty mimicries
        So true
        They almost woo
The hearer to believe he's singing too!
Speed me, Apollo: speed me, Artemis!
    And you, my dears, farewell! Remember me
Hereafter if, from any land that is,
    Some traveller question ye—
"Maidens, who was the sweetest man of speech
Fared hither, ever chanted on this beach?"
        I you beseech
Make answer to him, civilly—
"Sir, he was just a blind man, and his home
    In rocky Chios. But his songs were best,
And shall be ever in the days to come."
    Say that: and as I quest
In fair wall'd cities far, I'll tell them there
        (They'll list, for 'twill be true)
        Of Delos and of you.
But chief and evermore my song shall be
Of Prince Apollo, lord of Archery.
God of the Silver Bow, whom Leto bare—
    Leto, the lovely-tress'd.

Did time permit, I might quote you a chorus of
Aeschylus, a passage from Thucydides or from Aristotle,
to illustrate Gibbon's saying that the Greek language
"gave a soul to the objects of sense, and a body to the
abstractions of metaphysics." But there it is, and it
has haunted our literature; at first filtering through
Latin, at length breaking from Constantinople in flood

and led to us, to Oxford and Cambridge, by Erasmus, by Grocyn:

> Thee, that lord of splendid lore
> Orient from old Hellas' shore.

To have a sense of Greek, too, is such a corrective of taste. I quote another old schoolmaster here—a dead friend, Sidney Irwin:

What the Greeks disliked was extravagance, caprice, boastfulness, and display of all kinds. . . . The Greeks *hated* all monsters. The quaint phrase in the *Odyssey* about the Queen of the Laestrygones—"She was tall as a mountain, and they hated her"—would have seemed to them most reasonable. . . .

To read Greek is to have a perpetual witness to the virtue of pruning—of condensing—a perpetual protest against all that crowds, and swells, and weakens the writer's purpose. To forget this is but to "confound our skill in covetousness." We cannot all be writers . . . but we all wish to have good taste, and good taste is born of a generous caution about letting oneself go. I say *generous*, for caution is seldom generous—but it is a generous mood which is in no haste to assert itself. To consider the thing, the time, the place, the person, and to take yourself and your own feelings *only fifth* is to be armour-proof against bad taste.

VIII

They tell us that Greek is going, here. Well, I hold no brief for compulsory Greek; and I shall say but one word on it. I put it, rather idly, to a vote in a Cambridge Combination Room, the other day, and was amazed to find how the votes were divided. The men of science were by no means unanimous. They owned

that there was much to be said even for compulsory
Greek, if only Greek had been intelligently taught.
And with that, of course, I agree: for to learn Greek is,
after all, a baptism into a noble cult.   The Romans
knew *that*.   I believe that, even yet, if the schools
would rebuild their instruction in Greek so as to make
it interesting, as it ought to be, from the first, we should
oust those birds who croak and chatter upon the walls
of our old universities.   I find the following in Fitz-
Gerald's *Polonius:*

An old ruinous church which had harboured innumerable
jackdaws, sparrows, and bats, was at length repaired.
When the masons left it, the jackdaws, sparrows, and bats
came back in search of their old dwellings.   But these were
all filled up.   "Of what use now is this great building?"
said they, "come let us forsake this useless stone-heap."

And the beauty of this little apologue is that you can
read it either way.

IX

But, although a student of English Literature be
ignorant of Greek and Latin as languages, may he not
have Greek and Latin literature widely opened to him
by intelligent translations?   The question has often
been asked but I ask it again.   May not *some* translations open a door to him by which he can see them
through an atmosphere, and in that atmosphere the
authentic ancient gods walking: so that returning upon
English literature he may recognise them there, too,
walking and talking in a garden of values?   The highest

poetical speech of any one language defies, in my belief, translation into any other.   But Herodotus loses little, and North is every whit as good as Plutarch.

> Sigh no more, ladies; ladies, sigh no more!
>   Men were deceivers ever;
> One foot in sea and one on shore,
>   To one thing constant never

Suppose that rendered thus:

I enjoin upon the adult female population (γυναῖκες), not once but twice, that there be from this time forward, a total cessation of sighing.   The male is, and has been, constantly addicted to inconstancy, treading the ocean and the main-land respectively with alternate feet.

That, more or less, is what Paley did upon Euripides, and how would you like it if a modern Greek did it upon Shakespeare?   None the less I remember that my own first awed surmise of what Greek might mean came from a translated story of Herodotus—the story of Cleobis and Biton—at the tail of an old grammar-book, before I had learnt the Greek alphabet; and I am sure that the instinct of the old translators was sound; that somehow (as Wordsworth says somewhere) the present must be balanced on the wings of the past and the future, and that as you stretch out the one you stretch out the other to strength.

X

There is no derogation of new things in this plea I make specially to you who may be candidates in our

School of English.   You may remember my reading to
you in a previous lecture that liberal poem of Cory's
invoking the spirit of "dear divine Comatas," that

> Two minds shall flow together, the English and the Greek.

Well, I would have your minds, as you read out literature, reach back to that Dorian shepherd through an
atmosphere—his made ours—as through veils, each veil
unfolding a value.   So you will recognise how, from
Chaucer down, our literature has panted after the Mediterranean water-brooks.   So through an atmosphere
you will link (let me say) Collin's *Ode to Evening*, or
Matthew Arnold's *Strayed Reveller* up to the *Pervi-
gilium Veneris*, Mr. Sturge Moore's *Sicilian Vine-
dresser* up to Theocritus, Pericles' funeral oration down
to Lincoln's over the dead at Gettysburg.   And as I
read you just now some part of an English oration in
the Latin manner, so I will conclude with some stanzas
in the Greek manner.   They are by Landor—a proud
promise by a young writer, hopeful as I could wish any
young learner here to be.   The title—

Corinna, from Athens, to Tanagra

Tanagra! think not I forget
   Thy beautifully storied streets;
Be sure my memory bathes yet
   In clear Thermodon, and yet greets
The blithe and liberal shepherd-boy,
Whose sunny bosom swells with joy
When we accept his matted rushes
Upheav'd with sylvan fruit; away he bounds, and blushes.

A gift I promise: one I see
   Which thou with transport wilt receive,
The only proper gift for thee,
   Of which no mortal shall bereave
In later times thy mouldering walls,
Until the last old turret falls;
   A crown, a crown from Athens won,
A crown no god can wear, beside Latona's son.

There may be cities who refuse
   To their own child the honours due,
And look ungently on the Muse;
   But ever shall those cities rue
The dry, unyielding, niggard breast,
Offering no nourishment, no rest,
   To that young head which soon shall rise
Disdainfully, in might and glory, to the skies.

Sweetly where cavern'd Dirce flows
   Do white-arm'd maidens chaunt my **lay,**
Flapping the while with laurel-rose
   The honey-gathering tribes away;
And sweetly, sweetly Attic tongues
Lisp your Corinna's early songs;
   To her with feet more graceful come
The verses that have dwelt in kindred breasts at home.

O let thy children lean aslant
   Against the tender mother's knee,
And gaze into her face, and want
   To know what magic there can be
In words that urge some eyes to dance,
While others as in holy trance
   Look up to heaven: be such my praise!
Why linger? I must haste, or lose the Delphic bays.

ON READING THE BIBLE (I)

I

" *READ not to Contradict and Confute,*" says Bacon of Studies in general: and you may be the better disposed, Gentlemen, to forgive my choice of subject to-day if in my first sentence I rule *that* way of reading the Bible completely out of court. You may say at once that, the Bible being so full of doctrine as it is, and such a storehouse for exegesis as it has been, this is more easily said than profitably done. You may grant me that, the Scriptures in our Authorised Version are part and parcel of English Literature (and more than part and parcel); you may grant that a Professor of English Literature has therefore a claim, if not an obligation, to speak of them in that Version; you may— having granted my incessant refusal to disconnect our national literature from our national life, or to view them as disconnected—accept the conclusion which plainly flows from it; that no teacher of English can pardonably neglect what is at once the most majestic thing in our literature and by all odds the most spiritually living thing we inherit; in our courts at once superb monument and superabundant fountain of life; and yet you may discount beforehand what he must attempt.

For (say you) if he attempt the doctrine, he goes straight down to buffeted waters so broad that only stout theologians can win to shore; if, on the other hand, he ignore doctrine, the play is *Hamlet* with the Prince of Denmark left out. He reduces our Bible to "mere literature," to something "belletristic," pretty, an artifice, a flimsy, a gutted thing.

II

Now of all ways of dealing with literature that happens to be the way we should least admire. By that way we disassociate literature from life; "what they said" from the men who said it and meant it, not seldom at the risk of their lives. My pupils will bear witness in the memories that when we talk together concerning poetry, for example, by "poetry" we mean "that which the poets wrote," or (if you like) "the stuff the poets wrote"; and their intelligence tells them, of course, that any one who in the simple proposition "Poets wrote Poetry" connects an object with a subject by a verb does not, at any rate, intend to sunder what he has just been at pains, however slight, to join together: he may at least have the credit, whether he be right or wrong, of asserting his subject and his object to be interdependent. Take a particular proposition—John Milton wrote a poem called *Paradise Lost*. You will hardly contest the truth of that: but what does it mean? Milton wrote the story of the Fall of Man: he told it in some thousands of lines of decasyllabic verse unrhymed; he measured these lines out with exquisite cadences.

The object of our simple sentence includes all these, and this much beside: that he wrote the total poem and made it what it is. Nor can that object be fully understood—literature being, ever and always, so personal a thing—until we understand the subject, John Milton—what manner of man he was, and how on earth, being such a man, he contrived to do it. We shall never *quite* know that: but it is important we should get as near as we can.

Of the Bible this is yet more evident, it being a translation. Isaiah did not write the cadences of his prophecies, as we ordinary men of this country know them: Christ did not speak the cadences of the Parables or of the Sermon on the Mount, as we know them. These have been supplied by the translators. By all means let us study them and learn to delight in them; but Christ did not suffer for his cadences, still less for the cadences invented by Englishmen almost sixteen hundred years later; and Englishmen who went to the stake did not die for these cadences. They were Lollards and Reformers who lived too soon to have heard them; they were Catholics of the "old profession" who had either never heard or, having heard, abhorred them. These men were cheerful to die for the *meaning* of the Word and for its *authorship*—because it was spoken by Christ.

III

There is in fact, Gentlemen, no such thing as "mere literature." Pedants have coined that contemptuous term to express a figmentary concept of their own

imagination or—to be more accurate, an hallucination
of wrath—having about as much likeness to a *vera
causa* as had the doll which (if you remember) Maggie
Tulliver used to beat in the garret whenever, poor child,
the world went wrong with her somehow. The thoughts,
actions, and passions of men became literature by the
simple but difficult process of being recorded in memorable speech; but in that process neither the real thing
recorded nor the author is evacuated. *Belles lettres,
Fine Art* are odious terms, for which no clean-thinking
man has any use. There is no such thing in the world as
belles lettres; if there were, it would deserve the name.
As for *Fine Art,* the late Professor Butcher bequeathed
to us a translation of Aristotle's *Poetics* with some admirable appendixes—the whole entitled *Aristotle's
Theory of Poetry and Fine Art.* Aristotle never in his
life had a theory of Fine Art as distinct from other art:
nor (I wager) can you find in his discovered works a
word for any such thing. Now if Aristotle had a concept of "fine" art as distinguished from other art, he
was man enough to find a name for it. His omission
to do anything of the sort speaks for itself.

So you should beware of any teacher who would treat
the Bible or any part of it as "fine writing," mere
literature.

IV

Let me, having said this, at once enter a *caveat,* a
qualification. Although men do not go to the stake for
the cadences, the phrases of our Authorised Version, it

remains true that these cadences, these phrases, have
for three hundred years exercised a most powerful effect
upon their emotions. They do so by association of
ideas by the accreted memories of our race enwrapping
connotation around a word, a name—say the name
Jerusalem, or the name *Sion:*

> And they that wasted us, required of us mirth, saying,—
> Sing to us one of the songs of Sion.
> How shall we sing the Lord's song, in a strange land? If I
> forget thee, O Jerusalem, let my right hand forget her
> cunning!

It must be known to you, Gentlemen, that these
words can affect men to tears who never connect them
in thought with the actual geographical Jerusalem; who
connect it in thought merely with a quite different native home from which they are exiles. Here and there
some one man may feel a similar emotion over Landor's

> Tanagra, think not I forget . . .

But the word Jerusalem will strike twenty men twenty-
fold more poignantly: for to each it names the city
familiar in spirit to his parents when they knelt, and
to their fathers before them: not only the city which
was his nursery and yet lay just beyond the landscape
seen from its window; its connotation includes not only
what the word "Rome" has meant, and ever must
mean, to thousands on thousands setting eyes for the
first time on *The City:* but it holds, too, some hint of
the New Jerusalem, the city of twelve gates before the
vision of which St. John fell prone:

10

> Ah, my sweet home, Hierusalem,
>   Would God I were in thee
> Thy Gardens and thy gallant walks
>   Continually are green:
> There grows such sweet and pleasant flowers
>   As nowhere else are seen.
> Quite through the streets with pleasant sound
>   The flood of Life doth flow;
> Upon whose banks on every side
>   The wood of Life doth grow . . .
>
> Our Lady sings *Magnificat*
>   With tones surpassing sweet:
> And all the virgins bear their part,
>   Sitting about her feet.
> Hierusalem, my happy home,
>   Would God I were in thee!
> Would God my woes were at an end,
>   Thy joys that I might see!

You cannot (I say) get away from these connotations accreted through your own memories and your fathers'; as neither can you be sure of getting free of any great literature in any tongue, once it has been written. Let me quote you a passage from Cardinal Newman [he is addressing the undergraduates of the Catholic University of Dublin]:

How real a creation, how *sui generis*, is the style of Shakespeare, or of the Protestant Bible and Prayer Book or of Swift, or of Pope, or of Gibbon, or of Johnson!

[I pause to mark how just this man can be to his great enemies. Pope was a Roman Catholic, you will remember; Gibbon an infidel.]

Even were the subject-matter without meaning, though in truth the style cannot really be abstracted from the sense, still the style would, on *that* supposition, remain as perfect and original a work as Euclid's *Elements* or a symphony of Beethoven.

And, like music, it has seized upon the public mind: and the literature of England is no longer a mere letter, printed in books and shut up in libraries, but it is a living voice, which has gone forth in its expressions and its sentiments into the world of men, which daily thrills upon our ears and syllables our thoughts, which speaks to us through our correspondents and dictates when we put pen to paper. Whether we will or no, the phraseology of Shakespeare, of the Protestant formularies, of Milton, of Pope, of Johnson's Table-talk, and of Walter Scott, have become a portion of the vernacular tongue, the household words, of which perhaps we little guess the origin, and the very idioms of our familiar conversation. . . . So tyrannous is the literature of a nation; it is too much for us. We cannot destroy or reverse it. . . . We cannot make it over again. It is a great work of man, when it is no work of God's. . . . We cannot undo the past. English Literature will ever *have been* Protestant.

V

I am speaking, then, to hearers who would read not to contradict and confute; who have an inherited sense of the English Bible; and who have, even as I, a store of associated ideas, to be evoked by any chance phrase from it; beyond this, nothing that can be called scholarship by any stretch of the term.

Very well, then: my first piece of advice *on reading the Bible* is that you do it.

I have, of course, no reason at all to suppose or

suggest that any member of this present audience omits
to do it. But some general observations are permitted
to an occupant of this Chair: and, speaking generally,
and as one not constitutionally disposed to lamentation
[in the book we are discussing, for example, I find
Jeremiah the contributor least to my mind], I do believe
that the young read the Bible less, and enjoy it less—
probably read it less, because they enjoy it less—than
their fathers did.

The Education Act of 1870, often in these days
too sweepingly denounced, did a vast deal of good
along with no small amount of definite harm. At the
head of the harmful effects must (I think) be set its
discouragement of Bible reading; and this chiefly
through its encouraging parents to believe that they
could henceforth hand over the training of their children to the State, lock, stock, and barrel. You all
remember the picture in Burns of *The Cotter's Saturday
Night:*

> The chearfu' supper done, wi' serious face,
>   They, round the ingle, form a circle wide;
> The sire turns o'er, wi' patriarchal grace,
>   The big ha'-Bible, ance his father's pride.
>   His bonnet rev'rently is laid aside,
> His lyart haffets wearing thin and bare;
>   Those strains that once did sweet in Zion glide,
> He wales a portion with judicious care,
> And "Let us worship God!" he says, with solemn air.

But you know that the sire bred on the tradition of
1870 and now growing grey, does nothing of that sort

on a Saturday night: that, Saturday being tub-night, he inclines rather to order them into the back-kitchen to get washed; that on Sunday morning, having seen them off to a place of worship, he inclines to sit down and read, in place of the Bible, his Sunday newspaper: that in the afternoon he again shunts them off to Sunday-school. Now—to speak first of the children—it is good for them to be tubbed on Saturday night; good for them also, I dare say, to attend Sunday-school on the following afternoon; but not good in so far as they miss to hear the Bible read by their parents and

Pure religion breathing household laws.

"Pure religion"?—Well perhaps that begs the question: and I dare say Burn's cotter when he waled "a portion with judicious care," waled it as often as not—perhaps oftener than not—to contradict and confute; that often he contradicted and confuted very crudely, very ignorantly. But we may call it simple religion anyhow, sincere religion, parental religion, household religion: and for a certainty no "lessons" in day-school or Sunday-school have, for tingeing a child's mind, an effect comparable with that of a religion pervading the child's home, present at bedside and board:

Here a little child I stand,
Heaving up my either hand;
Cold as paddocks tho' they be,
Here I lift them up to Thee;
For a benison to fall
On our meat and on us all.   Amen.

—permeating the house, subtly instilled by the very
accent of his father's and his mother's speech.   For the
grown man . . . I happen to come from a part of England where men, in all my days, have been curiously
concerned with religion and are yet so concerned; so
much that you can scarce take up a local paper and turn
to the correspondence column but you will find some
heated controversy raging over Free Will and Pre-
destination, the Validity of Holy Orders, Original Sin,
Redemption of the many or the few:

> Go it Justice, go it Mercy!
> Go it Douglas, go it Percy!

But the contestants do not write in the language their
fathers used.   They seem to have lost the vocabulary,
and to have picked up, in place of it, the jargon of the
Yellow Press, which does not tend to clear definition
on points of theology.   The mass of all this controversial
stuff is no more absurd, no more frantic, than it used
to be: but in language it has lost its dignity with its
homeliness.   It has lost the colouring of the Scriptures,
the intonation of the Scriptures, the Scriptural *habit*.

If I turn from it to a passage in Bunyan, I am con-
versing with a man who, though he has read few other
books, has imbibed and soaked the Authorised Version
into his fibres so that he cannot speak but Biblically.
Listen to this:

As to the situation of this town, it lieth just between the
two worlds, and the first founder, and builder of it, so far as

by the best, and most authentic records I can gather, was
one Shaddai; and he built it for his own delight. He made it
the mirror, and glory of all that he made, even the Top-
piece beyond anything else that he did in that country: yea,
so goodly a town was Mansoul, when first built, that it is
said by some, the Gods at the setting up thereof, came down
to see it, and sang for joy. . . .

The wall of the town was well built, yea so fast and firm
was it knit and compact together, that had it not been for
the townsmen themselves, they could not have been shaken,
or broken for ever.

Or take this:

Now as they were going along and talking, they espied a
Boy feeding his Father's Sheep. The Boy was in very mean
Cloaths, but of a very fresh and well-favoured Countenance,
and as he sate by himself he Sung. . . . Then said their
Guide, Do you hear him? I will dare to say, that this Boy
lives a merrier Life, and wears more of that Herb called
Heart's-ease in his Bosom, than he that is clad in Silk and
Velvet.

I choose ordinary passages, not solemn ones in which
Bunyan is consciously scriptural. But you cannot miss
the accent.

That is Bunyan, of course; and I am far from saying
that the labouring men among whom I grew up, at the
fishery or in the hayfield, talked with Bunyan's magic.
But I do assert that they had something of the accent;
enough to be *like*, in a child's mind, the fishermen and
labourers among whom Christ found his first disciples.
They had the large simplicity of speech, the cadence,
the accent. But let me turn to Ireland, where, though

not directly derived from our English Bible a similar
scriptural accent survives among the peasantry and is,
I hope, ineradicable. I choose two sentences from a
book of "Memories" recently written by the survivor
of the two ladies who together wrote the incomparable
"Irish R.M." The first was uttered by a small culti-
vator who was asked why his potato-crop had failed:

"I couldn't hardly say" was the answer. "Whatever it
was, God spurned them in a boggy place."

Is that not the accent of Isaiah?

He will surely violently turn and toss thee like a ball into
a large country.

The other is the benediction bestowed upon the late
Miss Violet Martin by a beggar-woman in Skibbereen:

Sure ye're always laughing! That ye may laugh in the
sight of the Glory of Heaven!

VI

But one now sees, or seems to see, that we children
did, in our time, read the Bible a great deal, if perforce we were taught to read it in sundry bad ways: of
which perhaps the worst was that our elders hammered
in all the books, all the parts of it as equally inspired
and therefore equivalent. Of course this meant among
other things that they hammered it all in literally: but
let us not sentimentalise over that. It really did no

child any harm to believe that the universe was created
in a working week of six days, and that God sat down
and looked at it on Sunday, and behold it was very
good. A week is quite a long while to a child, yet a
definite division rounding off a square job. The bath-
taps at home usually, for some unexplained reason, went
wrong during the week-end: the plumber came in on
Monday and carried out his tools on Saturday at mid-
day. These little analogies really do (I believe) help the
infant mind, and not at all to its later detriment. Nor
shall I ask you to sentimentalise overmuch upon the
harm done to a child by teaching him that the bloodthirsty jealous Jehovah of the Book of Joshua is as
venerable (being one and the same unalterably, "with
whom is no variableness, neither shadow of turning")
as the Father "the same Lord, whose property is always
to have mercy," revealed to us in the Gospel, invoked
for us at the Eucharist. I do most seriously hold it to
be fatal if we grow up and are fossilised in any such
belief. (Where have we better proof than in the invo-
cations which the family of the Hohenzollerns have
been putting up, any time since August, 1914—and for
years before—to this bloody identification of the
Christian man's God with Joshua's?) My simple advice
is that you not only read the Bible early but read it
again and again: and if on the third or fifth reading it
leave you just where the first left you—if you still get
from it no historical sense of a race *developing* its concept of God—well then, the point of the advice is lost,
and there is no more to be said. But over this business

of teaching the Book of Joshua to children I am in some doubt. A few years ago an Education Committee, of which I happened to be Chairman, sent ministers of religion about, two by two, to test the religious instruction given in Elementary Schools. Of the two who worked around my immediate neighbourhood, one was a young priest of the Church of England, a mediævalist with an ardent passion for ritual; the other a gentle Congregational minister, a mere holy and humble man of heart. They became great friends in the course of these expeditions, and they brought back this report— "It is positively wicked to let these children grow up being taught that there is no difference in value between Joshua and St. Matthew: that the God of the Lord's Prayer is the same who commanded the massacre of Ai." Well, perhaps it is. Seeing how bloodthirsty old men can be in these days, one is tempted to think that they can hardly be caught too young and taught decency, if not mansuetude. But I do not remember, as a child, feeling any horror about it, or any difficulty in reconciling the two concepts. Children *are* a bit bloodthirsty, and I observe that two volumes of the late Captain Mayne Reid—*The Rifle Rangers*, and *The Scalp Hunters*—have just found their way into *The World's Classics* and are advertised alongside of Ruskin's *Sesame and Lilies* and the *De Imitatione Christi*, I leave you to think this out; adding but this for a suggestion: that as the Hebrew outgrew his primitive tribal beliefs, so the bettering mind of man casts off the old clouts of primitive doctrine, he being in fact better than his religion.

You have all heard preachers trying to show that Jacob was a better fellow than Esau somehow. You have all, I hope, rejected every such explanation. Esau was a gentleman: Jacob was not. The mind of a young man meets that wall, and there is no passing it. Later, the mind of the youth perceives that the writer of Jacob's history has a tribal mind and supposes throughout that for the advancement of his tribe many things are permissible and even admirable which a later and urbaner mind rejects as detestably sharp practice. And the story of Jacob becomes the more valuable to us historically as we realise what a hero he is to the bland chronicler.

VII

But of another thing, Gentlemen, I am certain: that we were badly taught in that these books, while preached to us as equivalent, were kept in separate compartments. We were taught the books of Kings and Chronicles as history. The prophets were the Prophets, inspired men predicting the future—which they only did by chance, as every inspired man does. Isaiah was never put into relation with his time at all; which means everything to our understanding of Isaiah, whether of Jerusalem or of Babylon. We ploughed through Kings and Chronicles, and made out lists of rulers, with dates and capital events. Isaiah was all fine writing about nothing at all, and historically we were concerned with him only to verify some far-fetched

reference to the Messiah in this or that Evangelist.
But there is not, never has been, really fine literature—
like Isaiah—composed about nothing at all: and in the
mere matter of prognostication I doubt if such experts
as Zadkiel and Old Moore have anything to fear from
any School of Writing we can build up in Cambridge.
But if we had only been taught to read Isaiah concurrently with the Books of the Kings, what a fire it would
have kindled among the dry bones of our studies!

Then said the Lord unto Isaiah, Go forth now to meet
Ahaz, thou, and Shear-jashub thy son, at the end of the
conduit of the upper pool in the highway of the fuller's field.

Scholars, of course, know the political significance of
that famous meeting. But if we had only known it; if
we had only been taught what Assyria was—with its
successive monarchs Tiglath-pileser, Shalmaneser, Sar-
gon, Sennacherib; and why Syria and Israel and Egypt
were trying to cajole or force Judah into alliance;
what a difference (I say) this passage would have
meant to us!

VIII

I daresay, after all, that the best way is not to bother
a boy too early and overmuch with history; that the
best way is to let him ramp at first through the Scriptures even as he might through *The Arabian Nights:* to
let him take the books as they come, merely indicating,
for instance, that Job is a great poem, the Psalms great

lyrics, the story of Ruth a lovely idyll, the Song of
Songs the perfection of an Eastern love-poem. Well,
and what then? He will certainly get less of *The Cotter's
Saturday Night* into it, and certainly more of the truth
of the East. There he will feel the whole splendid
barbaric story for himself: the flocks of Abraham and
Laban: the trek of Jacob's sons to Egypt for corn: the
figures of Rebekah at the well, Ruth at the gleaning,
and Rispah beneath the gibbet: Sisera bowing in weari-
ness: Saul—great Saul—by the tent-prop with the
jewels in his turban:

All its lordly male-sapphires, and rubies courageous at
heart.

Or consider—to choose one or two pictures out of the
tremendous procession—consider Michal, Saul's royal
daughter: how first she is given in marriage to David
to be a snare for him; how loving him she saves his life,
letting him down from the window and dressing up an
image on the bed in his place: how, later, she is handed
over to another husband Phaltiel, how David demands
her back, and she goes:

And her husband (Phaltiel) went with her along weeping
behind her to Bahurim. Then said Abner unto him, Go,
return. And he returned.

Or, still later, how the revulsion takes her, Saul's
daughter, as she sees David capering home before the
ark, and how her affection had done with this emotional

man of the ruddy countenance, so prone to weep in his
bed:

And as the ark of the Lord came into the city of David,
Michal Saul's daughter—

Mark the three words—

Michal Saul's daughter looked through a window, and saw
King David leaping and dancing before the Lord; and she
despised him in her heart.

The whole story goes into about ten lines. Your psycho-
logical novelist nowadays, given the wit to invent it,
would make it cover five hundred pages at least.

Or take the end of David in the first two chapters of
the First Book of Kings, with its tale of Oriental intrigues, plots, treacheries, murderings, in the depths of
the horrible palace wherein the old man is dying. Or
read of Solomon and his ships and his builders, and see
his Temple growing (as Heber put it) like a tall palm
with no sound of hammers. Or read again the end of
Queen Athaliah:

And when Athaliah heard the noise of the guard and of
the people, she came to the people into the temple of the
Lord.—And when she looked, behold, the king stood by a
pillar, as the manner was, and the princes and the trumpet-
ers by the king, and all the people of the land rejoiced, and
blew with trumpets: And Athaliah rent her clothes, and
cried Treason, Treason.—But Jehoiada the priest commanded the captains of the hundreds, the officers of the host,
and said unto them, Have her forth without the ranges. . . .
—And they laid hands on her; and she went by the way

by the which the horses came into the king's house: and
there was she slain.

Let a youngster read this, I say, just as it is written;
and how the true East—sound, scent, form, colour—
pours into the narrative!—cymbals and trumpets,
leagues of sand, caravans trailing through the heat,
priest and soldiery and kings going up between them to
the altar; blood at the foot of the steps, blood everywhere, smell of blood mingled with spices, sandal-wood,
dung of camels!

Yes, but how—if you will permit the word—how the
enjoyment of it as magnificent literature might be en-
hanced by a scholar who would condescend to whisper,
of his knowledge, the magical word here or there, to
the child as he reads! For an instance:

No child—no grown man with any sense of poetry—
can deny his ear to the Forty-fifth Psalm; the one that
begins "My heart is inditing a good matter," and
plunges into a hymn of royal nuptials. First (you remember) the singing-men, the sons of Korah, lift their
chant to the bridegroom, the King:

Gird thy sword upon thy thigh, O most mighty . . .
And in thy majesty ride prosperously.

Or as we hear it in the Book of Common Prayer:

Good luck have thou with thine honour . . .
—because of truth and meekness and righteousness; and
thy right hand shall teach thee terrible things. . . .
All thy garments smell of myrrh, and aloes, and cassia,

out of the ivory palaces, whereby they have made thee glad.

Anon they turn to the Bride:

Hearken, O daughter, and consider, and incline thine ear; forget also thine own people, and thy father's house. . . .
The King's daughter is all glorious within: her clothing is of wrought gold.
She shall be brought unto the king in raiment of needle-work: the virgins that be her fellows shall bear her company. And the daughter of Tyre shall be there with a gift. Instead of thy fathers shall be thy children, whom thou mayest make princes in all the earth.

For whom (wonders the young reader, spell-bound by this) for what happy bride and bridegroom was this glorious chant raised? Now suppose that, just here, he has a scholar ready to tell him what is likeliest true— that the bridegroom was Ahab—that the bride, the daughter of Sidon, was no other than Jezebel, and became what Jezebel now is—with what an awe of surmise would two other passages of the history, toll on his ear?

And one washed the chariot in the pool of Samaria; and the dogs licked up his blood. . . .
And when he (Jehu) was come in, he did eat and drink, and said, Go, see now this cursed woman, and bury her: for she is a king's daughter.
And they went to bury her: but they found no more of her than the skull, and the feet, and the palms of her hands.
Wherefore they came again, and told him. And he said, This is the word of the Lord, which he spake by his servant Elijah the Tishbite, saying, In the portion of Jezreel shall

dogs eat the flesh of Jezebel. . . so that (men) shall not say, This is Jezebel.

In another lecture, Gentlemen, I propose to take up the argument and attempt to bring it to this point. "How can we, having this incomparable work, *necessary* for study by all who would write English, bring it within the ambit of the English Tripos and yet avoid offending the experts?"

11

ON READING THE BIBLE (II)

I

WE left off last term, Gentlemen, upon a note of
protest. We wondered why it should be that
our English Version of the Bible lies under the ban of
schoolmasters, Boards of Studies, and all who devise
courses of reading and examinations in English Literature: that among our "prescribed books" we find
Chaucer's *Prologue*, we find *Hamlet*, we find *Paradise
Lost*, we find Pope's *Essay on Man*, again and again, but
The Book of Job never; *The Vicar of Wakefield* and
Gray's *Elegy* often, but *Ruth* or *Isaiah*, *Ecclesiasticus* or
Wisdom never.

I propose this morning:

(1) to enquire into the reasons for this, so far as I
can guess and interpret them;

(2) to deal with such reasons as we can discover or
surmise;

(3) to suggest to-day, some simple first aid: and in
another lecture, taking for experiment a single book
from the Authorised Version, some practical ways of
including it in the ambit of our new English Tripos.
This will compel me to be definite: and as definite proposals invite definite objections, by this method we are

likeliest to know where we are, and if the reform we seek be realisable or illusory.

II

I shall ask you then, first, to assent with me, that the Authorised Version of the Holy Bible is, as a literary achievement, one of the greatest in our language; nay, with the possible exception of the complete works of Shakespeare, the very greatest. You will certainly not deny this.

As little, or less, will you deny that more deeply than any other book—more deeply even than all the writings of Shakespeare—far more deeply—it has influenced our literature. Here let me repeat a short passage from a former lecture of mine (May 15, 1913, five years ago). I had quoted some few glorious sentences such as:

Thine eyes shall see the king in his beauty: they shall behold the land that is very far off.

And a man shall be as an hiding-place from the wind, and a covert from the tempest; as rivers of water in a dry place, as the shadow of a great rock in a weary land. . . .

So when this corruptible shall have put on incorruption and this mortal shall have put on immortality . . .

and having quoted these I went on:

When a nation has achieved this manner of diction, these rhythms for its dearest beliefs, a literature is surely established. . . . Wyclif, Tyndale, Coverdale and others before the forty-seven had wrought. The Authorised Version, setting a seal on all, set a seal on our national style. . . .

It has cadences homely and sublime, yet so harmonises them that the voice is always one Simple men—holy and humble men of heart like Isaak Walton and Bunyan—have their lips touched and speak to the homelier tune. Proud men, scholars—Milton, Sir Thomas Browne—practise the rolling Latin sentence; but upon the rhythms of our Bible they, too, fall back—"The great mutations of the world are acted, or time may be too short for our designs." "Acquaint thyself with the Choragium of the stars." "There is nothing immortal but immortality." The precise man Addison cannot excel one parable in brevity or in heavenly clarity: the two parts of Johnson's antithesis come to no more than this "Our Lord has gone up to the sound of a trump; with the sound of a trump our Lord has gone up." The Bible controls its enemy Gibbon as surely as it haunts the curious music of a light sentence of Thackeray's. It is in everything we see, hear, feel, because it is in us, in our blood.

If that be true, or less than gravely overstated: if the English Bible hold this unique place in our literature; if it be at once a monument, an example and (best of all) a well of English undefiled, no stagnant water, but quick, running, curative, refreshing, vivifying; may we not agree, Gentlemen, to require the weightiest reason why our instructors should continue to hedge in the temple and pipe the fountain off in professional conduits, forbidding it to irrigate freely our ground of study?

It is done so complacently that I do not remember to have met one single argument put up in defence of it; and so I am reduced to guess-work. What *can* be the justifying reason for an embargo on the face of it so silly and arbitrary, if not senseless?

III

Does it reside perchance in some primitive instinct of *taboo;* of a superstition of fetish-worship fencing off sacred things as unmentionable, and reinforced by the bad Puritan notion that holy things are by no means to be enjoyed?

If so, I begin by referring you to the Greeks and their attitude towards the Homeric poems. We, of course, hold the Old Testament more sacred than Homer. But I very much doubt if it be more sacred to us than the *Iliad* and the *Odyssey* were to an old Athenian, in his day. To the Greeks—and to forget this is the fruitfullest source of error in dealing with the Tragedians or even with Aristophanes—to the Greeks, their religion, such as it was, mattered enormously. They built their Theatre upon it, as we most certainly do not; which means that it had sunk into their daily life and permeated their enjoyment of it, as our religion certainly does not affect *our* life to enhance it as amusing or pleasurable. We go to Church on Sunday, and write it off as an observance; but if eager to be happy with a free heart, we close early and steal a few hours from the working-day. We antagonise religion and enjoyment, worship and holiday. Nature being too strong for any convention of ours, courtship has asserted itself as permissible on the Sabbath, if not as a Sabbatical institution.

Now the Greeks were just as much slaves to the letter of their Homer as any Auld Licht Elder to the letter of

St. Paul.　No one will accuse Plato of being over-
friendly to poetry.　Yet I believe you will find in Plato
some 150 direct citations from Homer, not to speak of
allusions scattered broadcast through the dialogues,
often as texts for long argument.　Of these citations and
allusions an inordinate number seem to us laboriously
trivial—that is to say, unless we put ourselves into the
Hellenic mind.　On the other hand Plato uses others
to enforce or illustrate his profoundest doctrines.　For
an instance, in *Phædo* (§ 96) Socrates is arguing that
the soul cannot be one with the harmony of the bodily
affections, being herself the master-player who commands the strings:

—almost always [he says] opposing and coercing them
in all sorts of ways throughout life, sometimes more violently with the pains of medicine and gymnastic; then
again more gently;—threatening, and also reprimanding the
desires, passions, fears, as if talking to a thing which is not
herself; as Homer in the *Odyssey* represents Odysseus doing
in the words

στῆθος δὲ πλήξας κραδίην ἠνίπαπε μύθῳ.
τέτλαθι δή, κραδίη·　καὶ κύντερον ἄλλο ποτ' ἔτλης.
He beat his breast, and thus reproached his heart:
Endure, my heart; far worse hast thou endured.

Do you think [asks Socrates] that Homer wrote this under
the idea that the soul is a harmony capable of being led by
the affections of the body, and not rather of a nature which
should lead and master them—herself a far diviner thing
than any harmony?

A Greek, then, will use Homer—*his* Bible—minutely
on niceties of conduct or broadly on first principles

of philosophy or religion. But equally, since it is
poetry all the time to him, he will take—or to instance
particular writers, Aristotle and the late Greek, Longinus will take—a single hexameter to illustrate a
minute trick of style or turn of phrase, as equally he
will choose a long passage or the whole *Iliad*, the whole
Odyssey, to illustrate a grand rule of poetic construction,
a first principle of æsthetics. For an example—"Herein," says Aristotle, starting to show that an Epic poem
must have Unity of Subject—"Herein, to repeat what
we have said before, we have a further proof of Homer's
superiority to the rest. He did not attempt to deal
even with the Trojan War in its entirety, though it
was a whole story with a definite beginning, middle, and
end—feeling apparently that it was too long a story
to be taken in at one view or else over-complicated by
variety of incidents." And as Aristotle takes the *Iliad*
—*his* Bible—to illustrate a grand rule of poetical construction, so the late writer of his tradition—Longinus—
will use it to exhibit the core and essence of poetical
sublimity; as in his famous ninth chapter, of which
Gibbon wrote:

The ninth chapter . . . [of the ΠΕΡΙΨΠΣΟΥΣ or *De
Sublimitate* of Longinus] is one of the finest monuments of
antiquity. Till now, I was acquainted only with two ways
of criticising a beautiful passage: the one, to show, by an
exact anatomy of it, the distinct beauties of it, and whence
they sprung; the other, an idle exclamation, or a general
encomium, which leaves nothing behind it. Longinus has
shown me that there is a third. He tells me his own feelings
upon reading it; and tells them with so much energy, that

he communicates them. I almost doubt which is more
sublime, Homer's Battle of the Gods, or Longinus's Apos-
trophe to Terentianus upon it.

Well, let me quote you, in translation, a sentence or
two from this chapter, which produced upon Gibbon
such an effect as almost to anticipate Walter Pater's
famous definition, "To feel the virtue of the poet, of
the painter, to disengage it, to set it forth—these are
the three stages of the critic's duty."

"Elsewhere," says Longinus, "I have written as follows:
Sublimity is the echo of a great soul."

"Sublimity is the echo of a great soul."—It was
worth repeating too—was it not?

For it is not possible that men with mean and servile
ideas and aims prevailing throughout their lives should
produce anything that is admirable and worthy of immortality. Great accents we expect to fall from the lips of
those whose thoughts are deep and grave. . . . Hear how
magnificently Homer speaks of the higher powers: "As
far as a man seeth with his eyes into the haze of distance as
he sitteth upon a cliff of outlook and gazeth over the wine-
dark sea, even so far at a bound leap the neighing horses of
the Gods."

"He makes" [says Longinus] "the vastness of the
world the measure of their leap." Then, after a criticism of the Battle of the Gods (too long to be quoted
here) he goes on:

Much superior to the passages respecting the Battle of the
Gods are those which represent the divine nature as it really

is—pure and great and undefiled; for example, what is said of Poseidon.

Her far-stretching ridges, her forest-trees, quaked in dismay,
And her peaks, and the Trojans' town, and the ships of
　Achaia's array,
Beneath his immortal feet, as onward Poseidon strode.
Then over the surges he drave: leapt, sporting before the
　God,
Sea-beasts that uprose all round from the depths, for their
　king they knew,
And for rapture the sea was disparted, and onward the car-
　steeds flew.[1]

Then how does Longinus conclude? Why, very strangely—very strangely indeed, whether you take the treatise to be by that Longinus, the Rhetorician and Zenobia's adviser, whom the Emperor Aurelian put to death, or prefer to believe it the work of an unknown hand in the first century. The treatise goes on:

Similarly, the legislator of the Jews [Moses], no ordinary man, having formed and expressed a worthy conception of the might of the Godhead, writes at the very beginning of his Laws, "God said"—What? "Let there be light, and there was light."

IV

So here, Gentlemen, you have Plato, Aristotle, Longinus—all Greeks of separate states—men of eminence all three, and two of surpassing eminence, all three and each in his time and turn treating Homer

[1] I borrow the verse and in part the prose of Professor W. Rhys Roberts' Translation.

reverently as Holy Writ and yet enjoying it liberally as poetry. For indeed the true Greek mind had no thought to separate poetry from religion, as to the true Greek mind reverence and liberty to enjoy, with the liberty of mind that helps to enjoy, were all tributes to the same divine thing. They had no professionals, no puritans, to hedge it off with a *taboo:* and so when the last and least of the three, Longinus, comes to *our* Holy Writ— the sublime poetry in which Christendom reads its God, his open mind at once recognises it as poetry and as sublime. "God said, Let there be light; and there was light." If Longinus could treat this as sublime poetry, why cannot we, who have translated and made it ours?

V

Are we forbidden on the ground that our Bible is directly inspired? Well, inspiration, as Sir William Davenant observed and rather wittily proved, in his Preface to *Gorboduc*, "is a dangerous term." It is dangerous mainly because it is a relative term, a term of degrees. You may say definitely of some things that the writer was inspired, as you may certify a certain man to be mad—that is, so thoroughly and convincingly mad that you can order him under restraint. But quite a number of us are (as they say in my part of the world) "not exactly," and one or two of us here and there at moments may have a touch even of inspiration. So of the Bible itself: I suppose that few nowadays would contend it to be all inspired *equally.* "No" you may say, "not all equally: but all of it *directly*, as no other book is."

To that I might answer, "How do you *know* that direct inspiration ceased with the Revelation of St. John the Divine, and closed the book.   It may be: but how do you know, and what authority have you to say that Wordsworth's *Tintern Abbey*, for example, or Browning's great Invocation of Love was not directly inspired? Certainly the men who wrote them were rapt above themselves: and, if not directly, why indirectly, and how?

But I pause on the edge of a morass, and spring back to firmer ground.   Our Bible, as we have it, is a translation, made by forty-seven men and published in the year 1611.   The original—and I am still on firm ground because I am quoting now from *The Cambridge History of English Literature*—"either proceeds from divine inspiration, as some will have it, or, according to others, is the fruit of the religious genius of the Hebrew race. From either point of view the authors are highly gifted individuals" [!]—

highly gifted individuals, who, notwithstanding their diversities, and the progressiveness observable in their representations of the nature of God, are wonderfully consistent in the main tenor of their writings, and serve, in general, for mutual confirmation and illustration.   In some cases, this may be due to the revision of earlier productions by later writers, which has thus brought more primitive conceptions into a degree of conformity with maturer and profounder views; but, even in such cases, the earlier conception often lends itself, without wrenching, to the deeper interpretation and the completer exposition. The Bible is not distinctively an intellectual achievement.

In all earnest I protest that to write about the Bible in such a fashion is to demonstrate inferentially that it has never quickened you with its glow; that, whatever your learning, you have missed what the unlearned Bunyan, for example, so admirably caught—the true *wit* of the book. The writer, to be sure, is dealing with the originals. Let us more humbly sit at the feet of the translators. "Highly gifted individuals," or no, the sort of thing the translators wrote was "And God said, Let there be light," "A sower went forth to sow," "The Kingdom of Heaven is like unto leaven which a woman took," "The wages of sin is death," "The trumpet shall blow," "Jesus wept," "Death is swallowed up in victory."

Let me quote you for better encouragement, as well as for relief, a passage from Matthew Arnold on the Authorised Version:

The effect of Hebrew poetry can be preserved and transferred in a foreign language as the effect of other great poetry cannot. The effect of Homer, the effect of Dante, is and must be in great measure lost in a translation, because their poetry is a poetry of metre, or of rhyme, or both; and the effect of these is not really transferable. A man may make a good English poem with the matter and thoughts of Homer and Dante, may even try to reproduce their metre or rhyme: but the metre and rhyme will be in truth his own, and the effect will be his, not the effect of Homer or Dante. Isaiah's, on the other hand, is a poetry, as is well known, of parallelism; it depends not on metre and rhyme, but on a balance of thought, conveyed by a corresponding balance of sentence; and the effect of this *can* be transferred to another language. . . . Hebrew poetry has in addition the effect of assonance and other effects which cannot perhaps be transferred; but its main effect, its effect of parallelism of thought and sentence, can.

I take this from the preface to his little volume in which Arnold confesses that his "paramount object is to get Isaiah enjoyed."

VI

Sundry men of letters besides Matthew Arnold have pleaded for a literary study of the Bible, and specially of our English Version, that we may thereby enhance our enjoyment of the work itself and, through this, enjoyment and understanding of the rest of English Literature, from 1611 down. Specially among these pleaders let me mention Mr. F. B. Money-Coutts (now Lord Latymer) and a Cambridge man, Dr. R. G. Moulton, now Professor of Literary Theory and Interpretation in the University of Chicago. Of both these writers I shall have something to say. But first and generally, if you ask me why all their pleas have not yet prevailed, I will give you my own answer—the fault as usual lies in ourselves—in our own tameness and incuriosity.

There is no real trouble with the *taboo* set up by professionals and puritans, if we have the courage to walk past it as Christian walked between the lions; no real tyranny we could not overthrow, if it were worth while, with a push; no need at all for us to "wreathe our sword in myrtle boughs." What tyranny exists has grown up through the quite well-meaning labours of quite well-meaning men: and, as I started this lecture by saying, I have never heard any serious reason given why we should not include portions of the English Bible in our English Tripos, if we choose.

> Nos te,
> Nos facimus, Scriptura, deam.

Then why don't we choose?

To answer this, we must (I suggest) seek somewhat further back. The Bible—that is to say the body of the old Hebrew Literature clothed for us in English— comes to us in our childhood. But how does it come?

Let me, amplifying a hint from Dr. Moulton, ask you to imagine a volume including the great books of our own literature all bound together in some such order as this: *Paradise Lost*, Darwin's *Descent of Man*, *The Anglo-Saxon Chronicle*, Walter Map, Mill *On Liberty*, Hooker's *Ecclesiastical Polity*, *The Annual Register*, Froissart, Adam Smith's *Wealth of Nations*, *Domesday Book*, *Le Morte d'Arthur*, Campbell's *Lives of the Lord Chancellors*, Boswell's *Johnson*, Barbour's *The Bruce*, Hakluyt's *Voyages*, Clarendon, Macaulay, the plays of Shakespeare, Shelley's *Prometheus Unbound*, *The Faerie Queene*, Palgrave's *Golden Treasury*, Bacon's *Essays*, Swinburne's *Poems and Ballads*, FitzGerald's *Omar Khayyàm*, Wordsworth, Browning, *Sartor Resartus*,

Burton's *Anatomy of Melancholy*, Burke's *Letters on a Regicide Peace*, Ossian, *Piers Plowman*, Burke's *Thoughts on the Present Discontents*, Quarles, Newman's *Apologia*, Donne's *Sermons*, Ruskin, Blake, *The Deserted Village*, *Manfred*, Blair's *Grave*, *The Complaint of Deor*, Bailey's *Festus*, Thompson's *Hound of Heaven*.

Will you next imagine that in this volume most of the author's names are lost; that, of the few that survive a number have found their way into wrong places; that Ruskin for example is credited with *Sartor Resartus;* that *Laus Veneris* and *Dolores* are ascribed to Queen Elizabeth, *The Anatomy of Melancholy* to Charles II; and that, as for the titles, these were never invented by the authors, but by a Committee?

Will you still go on to imagine that all the poetry is printed as prose; while all the long paragraphs of prose are broken up into short verses, so that they resemble the little passages set out for parsing or analysis in an examination paper?

This device, as you know, was first invented by the exiled translators who published the Geneva Bible (as it is called) in 1557; and for pulpit use, for handiness of reference, for "waling a portion," it has its obvious advantages: but it is, after all and at the best, a very primitive device: and, for my part, I consider it the deadliest invention of all for robbing the book of outward resemblance to literature and converting it to the aspect of a gazetteer—a *biblion a-biblion*, as Charles Lamb puts it.

Have we done? By no means. Having effected all

this, let us pepper the result over with italics and
numerals, print it in double columns, with a marginal
gutter on either side, each gutter pouring down an inky
flow of references and cross references. Then, and not
till then, is the outward disguise complete—so far as
you are concerned. It remains only then to appoint it
to be read in Churches, and oblige the child to get
selected portions of it by heart on Sundays. But you
are yet to imagine that the authors themselves have
taken a hand in the game: that the later ones suppose
all the earlier ones to have been predicting all the
time in a nebulous fashion what they themselves have
to tell, and indeed to have written mainly with that
object: so that Macaulay and Adam Smith, for example,
constantly interrupt the thread of their discourse to
affirm that what they tell us must be right because
Walter Map or the author of *Piers Plowman* foretold
it ages before.

Now a grown man—that is to say, a comparatively
unimpressionable man—that is again to say, a man past
the age when to enjoy the Bible is priceless—has probably found out somehow that the word prophet does
not (in spite of vulgar usage) mean "a man who pre-
dicts." He has experienced too many prophets of that
kind—especially since 1914—and he respects Isaiah
too much to rank Isaiah among them. He has been in
love, belike; he has read the Song of Solomon: he very
much doubts if, on the evidence, Solomon was the kind
of lover to have written that Song, and he is quite
certain that when the lover sings to his beloved:

Thy two breasts are like two young roes that are twins.
Thy neck is as a tower of ivory; thine eyes like the fishpools
in Heshbon, by the gate of Bath-rabbim.

—he knows, I say, that this is not a description of the
Church and her graces, as the chapter-heading auda-
ciously asserts.   But he is lazy; too lazy even to com-
mend the Revised Version for striking Solomon out of
the Bible, calling the poem The Song of Songs, omitting
the absurd chapter-headings, and printing the poetry as
poetry ought to be printed.   The old-fashioned arrangement was good enough for him.   Or he goes to church
on Christmas Day and listens to a first lesson, of which
the old translators made nonsense, and, in two passages
at least, stark nonsense.   But, again, the old nonsense is
good enough for him; soothing in fact.   He is not even
quite sure that the Bible, looking like any other book,
ought to be put in the hands of the young.

In all this I think he is wrong.   I am sure he is wrong
if our contention be right, that the English Bible should
be studied by us all for its poetry and its wonderful
language as well as for its religion—the religion and
the poetry being in fact inseparable.   For then, in
Euripides's phrase, we should clothe the Bible in a dress
through which its beauty might best shine.

VII

If you ask me How?   I answer—first begging you to
bear in mind that we are planning the form of the book
for our purpose, and that other forms will be used for

other purposes—that we should start with the simplest
alterations, such as these:

(1) The books should be re-arranged in their right
order, so far as this can be ascertained (and much of it
has been ascertained). I am told, and I can well believe
that this would at a stroke clear away a mass of con-
fusion in strictly Biblical criticism. But that is not my
business. I know that it would immensely help our
literary study.

(2) I should print the prose continuously, as prose
is ordinarily and properly printed: and the poetry in
verse lines, as poetry is ordinarily and properly printed.
And I should print each on a page of one column, with
none but the necessary notes and references, and these
so arranged that they did not tease and distract the eye.

(3) This arrangement should be kept, whether for
the Tripos we prescribe a book in the Authorised text
or in the Revised. As a rule, perhaps—or as a rule for
some years to come—we shall probably rely on the
Authorised Version: but for some books (and I instance
Job) we should undoubtedly prefer the Revised.

(4) With the verse we should, I hold, go farther even
than the Revisers. As you know, much of the poetry
in the Bible, especially of such as was meant for music,
is composed in stanzaic form, or in strophe and anti-
strophe, with prelude and conclusion, sometimes with
a choral refrain. We should print these, I contend, in
their proper form, just as we should print an English
poem in its proper form.

I shall conclude to-day with a striking instance of

this, with four strophes from the 107th Psalm, taking leave to use at will the Authorised, the Revised and the Coverdale Versions. Each strophe you will note, has a double refrain. As Dr. Moulton points out, the one puts up a cry for help, the other an ejaculation of praise after the help has come. Each refrain has a sequel verse, which appropriately changes the motive and sets that of the next stanza:

(i)

They wandered in the wilderness in a solitary way;
They found no city to dwell in.
Hungry and thirsty,
Their soul fainted in them.
   Then they cried unto the Lord in their trouble,
   And he delivered them out of their distresses.
He led them forth by a straight way,
That they might go to a city of habitation.
   Oh that men would praise the Lord for his goodness,
   And for his wonderful works to the children of men!
For he satisfieth the longing soul,
And filleth the hungry soul with goodness.

(ii)

Such as sit in darkness, and in the shadow of death,
Being bound in affliction and iron;
Because they rebelled against the words of God,
And contemned the counsel of the most High:
Therefore he brought down their heart with labour;
They fell down, and there was none to help.
   Then they cried unto the Lord in their trouble,
   And he saved them out of their distresses.
He brought them out of darkness and the shadow of death,
And brake their bands in sunder.

Oh that men would praise the Lord for his goodness,
And for his wonderful works to the children of men!
For he hath broken the gates of brass,
And cut the bars of iron in sunder.

(iii)

Fools because of their transgression,
And because of their iniquities, are afflicted,
Their soul abhorreth all manner of meat;
And they draw near unto death's door.
    Then they cry unto the Lord in their trouble,
    And he saveth them out of their distresses.
He sendeth his word and healeth them,
And delivereth them from their destructions.
    Oh that men would praise the Lord for his goodness,
    And for his wonderful works to the children of men!
And let them offer the sacrifices of thanksgiving,
And declare his works with singing!

(iv)

They that go down to the sea in ships,
That do business in great waters;
These see the works of the Lord,
And his wonders in the deep.
For he commandeth, and raiseth the stormy wind,
Which lifteth up the waves thereof.
They mount up to the heaven,
They go down again to the depths;
Their soul melteth away because of trouble.
They reel to and fro,
And stagger like a drunken man,
And are at their wits' end.
    Then they cry unto the Lord in their trouble,
    And he bringeth them out of their distresses.
He maketh the storm a calm,
So that the waves thereof are still.

Then are they glad because they be quiet;
So he bringeth them unto the haven where they would be.
Oh that men would praise the Lord for his goodness,
And for his wonderful works to the children of men!
Let them exalt him also in the assembly of the people,
And praise him in the seat of the elders!

ON READING THE BIBLE (III)

I

MY task to-day, Gentlemen, is mainly practical: to choose a particular book of Scripture and show (if I can) not only that it deserves to be enjoyed, in its English rendering, as a literary masterpiece, because it abides in that dress, an indisputable classic for us, as surely as if it had first been composed in English; but that it can, for purposes of study, serve the purpose of any true literary school of English as readily, and as usefully, as the Prologue to *The Canterbury Tales* or *Hamlet* or *Paradise Lost*. I shall choose *The Book of Job* for several reasons, presently to be given; but beg you to understand that, while taking it for a striking illustration, I use it but to illustrate; that what may be done with *Job* may, in degree, be done with *Ruth*, with *Esther*, with the *Psalms*, *The Song of Songs*, *Ecclesiastes;* with Isaiah of Jerusalem, Ezekiel, sundry of the prophets; even with St. Luke's Gospel or St. Paul's letters to the Churches.

My first reason, then, for choosing *Job* has already been given. It is the most striking illustration to be found. Many of the Psalms touch perfection as lyrical strains: of the ecstacy of passion in love I suppose *The*

Song of Songs to express the very last word. There are chapters of Isaiah that snatch the very soul and ravish it aloft. In no literature known to me are short stories told with such sweet austerity of art as in the Gospel parables—I can even imagine a high and learned artist in words, after rejecting them as divine on many grounds, surrendering in the end to their divine artistry. But for high seriousness combined with architectonic treatment on a great scale; for sublimity of conception, working malleably within a structure which is simple, severe, complete, having a beginning, a middle and an end; for diction never less than adequate, constantly right and therefore not seldom superb, as theme, thought, and utterance soar up together and make one miracle, I can name no single book of the Bible to compare with *Job*.

My second reason is that the poem, being brief, compendious and quite simple in structure, can be handily expounded; *Job* is what Milton precisely called it, "a brief model." And my third reason (which I must not hide) is that two writers whom I mentioned in my last lecture—Lord Latymer and Professor R. G. Moulton—have already done this for me. A man who drives at practice must use the tools other men have made, so he use them with due acknowledgment; and this acknowledgment I pay by referring you to Book II of Lord Latymer's *The Poet's Charter*, and to the analysis of *Job* with which Professor Moulton introduces his *Literary Study of the Bible*.

II

But I have a fourth reason, out of which I might make an apparent fifth by presenting it to you in two different ways. Those elders of you who have followed certain earlier lectures "On the Art of Writing" may remember that they set very little store upon metre as a dividing line between poetry and prose, and no store at all upon rhyme. I am tempted to-day to go farther, and to maintain that, the larger, the sublimer, your subject is, the more impertinent rhyme becomes to it: and that this impertinence increases in a sort of geometrical progression as you advance from monosyllabic to dissyllabic and on to trisyllabic rhyme. Let me put this by a series of examples.

We start with no rhyme at all:

> Hail, holy Light, offspring of Heaven first born!
> Or of the Eternal coeternal beam
> May I express thee unblamed? since God is light,
> And never but in unapproached light
> Dwelt from eternity.

We feel of this, as we feel of a great passage in *Hamlet* or *Lear*, that here is verse at once capable of the highest sublimity and capable of sustaining its theme, of lifting and lowering it at will, with endless resource in the slide and pause of the cæsura, to carry it on and on. We feel it to be adequate, too, for quite plain straightforward narrative, as in this passage from *Balder Dead:*

> But from the hill of Lidskialf Odin rose,
> The throne, from which his eye surveys the world;

And mounted Sleipner, and in darkness rode
To Asgard. And the stars came out in heaven,
High over Asgard, to light home the King.
But fiercely Odin gallop'd, moved in heart;
And swift to Asgard, to the gate, he came.
And terribly the hoofs of Sleipner rang
Along the flinty floor of Asgard streets,
And the Gods trembled on their golden beds—
Hearing the wrathful Father coming home—
For dread, for like a whirlwind, Odin came.
And to Valhalla's gate he rode, and left
Sleipner; and Sleipner went to his own stall:
And in Valhalla Odin laid him down.

Now of rhyme he were a fool who, with Lycidas, or
Gray's *Elegy*, or certain choruses of *Prometheus Unbound*, or page after page of Victor Hugo in his mind,
should assert it to be in itself inimical, or a hindrance,
or even less than a help, to sublimity; or who, with
Dante in his mind, should assert it to be, in itself, any
bar to continuous and sustained sublimity. But languages differ vastly in their wealth of rhyme, and differ
out of any proportion to their wealth in words: English
for instance being infinitely richer than Italian in vocabulary, yet almost ridiculously poorer in dissyllabic,
or feminine rhymes. Speaking generally, I should say
that in proportion to its wonderful vocabulary, English
is poor even in single rhymes; that the words "love,"
"truth," "God," for example have lists of possible con-
geners so limited that the mind, hearing the word
"love," runs forward to match it with "dove" or
"above" or even with "move": and this gives it a
sense of arrest, of listening, of check, of waiting, which

alike impedes the flow of Pope in imitating Homer, and
of Spenser in essaying a sublime and continuous story
of his own. It does well enough to carry Chaucer over
any gap with a "forsooth as I you say" or "forsooth as I you tell": but it does so at a total cost of the
sublime. And this (I think) was really at the back of
Milton's mind when in the preface to *Paradise Lost* he
championed blank verse against "the jingling sound of
like endings."

But when we pass from single rhymes to double, of
which Dante had an inexhaustible store, we find the
English poet almost a pauper; so nearly a pauper that
he has to achieve each new rhyme by a trick—which
tricking is fatal to rapture, alike in the poet and the
hearer. Let me instance a poem which, planned for
sublimity, keeps tumbling flat upon earth through the
inherent fault of the machine—I mean Myers's *St. Paul*
—a poem which, finely conceived, pondered, worked
and re-worked upon in edition after edition, was from
the first condemned (to my mind) by the technical
bar of dissyllabic rhyme which the poet unhappily
chose. I take one of its most deeply felt passages—
that of St. Paul protesting against his conversion
being taken for instantaneous, wholly accounted for
by the miraculous vision related in the *Acts of the
Apostles:*

Let no man think that sudden in a minute
  All is accomplished and the work is done;—
Though with thine earliest dawn thou shouldst begin it
  Scarce were it ended in thy setting sun.

Oh the regret, the struggle and the failing!
　　Oh the days desolate and useless years!
Vows in the night, so fierce and unavailing!
　　Stings of my shame and passion of my tears!

How have I seen in Araby Orion,
　　Seen without seeing, till he set again,
Known the night-noise and thunder of the lion,
　　Silence and sounds of the prodigious plain!

How have I knelt with arms of my aspiring
　　Lifted all night in irresponsive air,
Dazed and amazed with overmuch desiring,
　　Blank with the utter agony of prayer!

"What," ye will say, "and thou who at Damascus
　　Sawest the splendour, answeredst the Voice;
So hast thou suffered and canst dare to ask us,
　　Paul of the Romans, bidding us rejoice?"

You cannot say I have instanced a passage anything short of fine. But do you not feel that a man who is searching for a rhyme to Damascus has not really the time to cry "Abba, father"? Is not your own rapture interrupted by some wonder "How will he bring it off"? And when he has searched and contrived to "ask us," are we responsive to the ecstasy? Has he not—if I may employ an Oriental trope for once—let in the chill breath of cleverness upon the garden of beatitude? No man can be clever and ecstatic at the same moment.[1]

As for triple rhymes—rhymes of the comedian who had a lot o' news with many curious facts about the

[1] It is fair to say that Myers cancelled the Damascus stanza in his final edition.

square on the hypotenuse, or the cassiowary who ate
the missionary on the plains of Timbuctoo, with Bible,
prayer-book, hymn-book too—they are for the facetious
and removed, as far as geometrical progression can
remove them, from any *Paradise Lost* or *Regained*.

It may sound a genuine note, now and then:

> Alas! for the rarity
> Of Christian charity
> Under the sun!
> Oh, it was pitiful!
> Near a whole city full,
> Home she had none!

But not often: and, I think, never but in lyric.

III

So much, then, for rhyme. We will approach the
question of metre, helped or unhelped by rhyme, in
another way; and a way yet more practical.

When Milton (determined to write a grand epic)
was casting about for his subject, he had a mind for
some while, to attempt the story of *Job*. You may
find evidence for this in a MS. preserved here in Trinity
College Library. You will find printed evidence in a
passage of his *Reason of Church Government:*

"Time serves not now," he writes, "and perhaps I might
seem too profuse to give any certain account of what the
mind at home, in the spacious circuits of her musing, hath
liberty to propose to herself, though of highest hope and
hardest attempting; whether that epic form whereof the

two poems of Homer, and those other two of Virgil and
Tasso, are a diffuse, and the book of Job a brief model. . . ."

Again, we know *Job* to have been one of the three
stories meditated by Shelley as themes for great lyrical
dramas, the other two being the madness of Tasso and
Prometheus Unbound. Shelley never abandoned this
idea of a lyrical drama on Job; and if Milton abandoned
the idea of an epic, there are passages in *Paradise Lost* as
there are passages in *Prometheus Unbound* that might well
have been written for this other story. Take the lines

> Why am I mock'd with death, and lengthen'd out
> To deathless pain? How gladly would I meet
> Mortality my sentence, and be earth
> Insensible! how glad would lay me down
> As in my mother's lap! There I should rest
> And sleep secure; . . .

What is this, as Lord Latymer asks, but an echo of
Job's words?—

> For now should I have lien down and been quiet;
> I should have slept; then had I been at rest:
> With kings and counsellers of the earth,
> Which built desolate places for themselves . . .
> There the wicked cease from troubling;
> And there the weary be at rest.

There is no need for me to point out how exactly,
though from two nearly opposite angles, the story of
Job would hit the philosophy of Milton and the philosophy of Shelley to the very heart. What is the story
of the afflicted patriarch but a direct challenge to a
protestant like Milton (I use the word in its strict

sense) to justify the ways of God to man? It is the very
purpose, in sum, of the *Book of Job*, as it is the very
purpose, in sum, of *Paradise Lost:* and since both
poems can only work out the justification by long
argumentative speeches, both poems lamentably fail as
real solutions of the difficulty.   To this I shall recur,
and here merely observe that *qui s' excuse s' accuse:* a
God who can only explain himself by the help of long-
winded scolding, or of long-winded advocacy, though
he employ an archangel for advocate, has given away
the half of his case by the implicit admission that there
are two sides to the question.   And when we have put
aside the poetical ineptitude of a Creator driven to
apology, it remains that to Shelley the Jehovah, who,
for a sort of wager, allowed Satan to torture Job merely
for the game of testing him, would be no better than
any other tyrant; would be a miscreant Creator,
abominable as the Zeus of the *Prometheus Unbound.*

Now you may urge that Milton and Shelley dropped
Job for hero because both felt him to be a merely static
figure: and that the one chose Satan, the rebel angel,
the other chose Prometheus the rebel Titan, because
both are active rebels, and as epic and drama require
action, each of these heroes makes the thing move; that
Satan and Prometheus are not passive sufferers like Job
but souls as quick and fiery as Byron's Lucifer:

> Souls who dare use their immortality—
> Souls who dare look the Omnipotent tyrant in
> His everlasting face, and tell him that
> His evil is not good.

Very well, urge this: urge it with all your might. All
the while you will be doing just what I desire you to do,
using *Job* alongside *Prometheus Unbound* and *Paradise
Lost* as a comparative work of literature.

But, if you ask me for my own opinion why Milton
and Shelley dropped their intention to make poems on
the *Book of Job*, it is that they no sooner tackled it than
they found it to be a magnificent poem already, and a
poem on which, with all their genius, they found themselves unable to improve.

I want you to realise a thing most simple, demonstrable by five minutes of practice, yet so confused by
conventional notions of what poetry is that I dare say
it to be equally demonstrable that Milton and Shelley
discovered it only by experiment. Does this appear to
you a bold thing to say of so tremendous an artist as
Milton? Well, of course it would be cruel to quote in
proof his paraphrases of Psalms cxiv and cxxxvi: to set
against the Authorised Version's

> When Israel went out of Egypt,
>   The house of Jacob from a people of strange language

such pomposity as

> When the blest seed of Terah's faithful son
> After long toil their liberty had won—

or against

> O give thanks . . .
> To him that stretched out the earth above the waters:
>   for his mercy endureth for ever.
> To him that made great lights:
>   for his mercy endureth for ever

such stuff as

> Who did the solid earth ordain
> To rise above the watery plain;
> *For his mercies aye endure,*
> *Ever faithful, ever sure.*
>
> Who, by his all-commanding might,
> Did fill the new-made world with light;
> *For his mercies aye endure,*
> *Ever faithful, ever sure—*

verses yet farther weakened by the late Sir William Baker for *Hymns Ancient and Modern.*

It were cruel, I say, to condemn these attempts as little above those of Sternhold and Hopkins, or even of those of Tate and Brady: for Milton made them at fifteen years old, and he who afterwards consecrated his youth to poetry soon learned to know better. And yet, bearing in mind the passages in *Paradise Lost* and *Paradise Regained* which paraphrase the Scriptural narrative, I cannot forbear the suspicion that, though as an artist he had the instinct to feel it, he never quite won to *knowing* the simple fact that the thing had already been done and surpassingly well done: he, who did so much to liberate poetry from rhyme—he—even he who in the grand choruses of *Samson Agonistes* did so much to liberate it from strict metre—never quite realised, being hag-ridden by the fetish that rides between two panniers, the sacred and the profane, that this translation of *Job* already belongs to the category of poetry, *is* poetry, already above metre, and in rhythm

far on its way to the insurpassable.   If rhyme be allowed
to that greatest of arts, if metre, is not rhythm above
both for her service?   Hear in a sentence how this
poem uplifts the rhythm of the Vulgate:

> *Ecce, Deus magnus vincens sapientiam; numeros annorum
> ejus inestimabiles !*

But hear, in a longer passage, how our English rhythm
swings and sways to the Hebrew parallels:

Surely there is a mine for silver,
And a place for gold which they refine.
Iron is taken out of the earth,
And brass is molten out of the stone.
Man setteth an end to darkness,
And searcheth out to the furthest bound
The stones of thick darkness and of the shadow of death.
He breaketh open a shaft away from where men sojourn;
They are forgotten of the foot *that passeth by;*
They hang afar from men, they swing to and fro.
As for the earth, out of it cometh bread:
And underneath it is turned up as it were by fire
The stones thereof are the place of sapphires,
And it hath dust of gold.
That path no bird of prey knoweth,
Neither hath the falcon's eye seen it:
The proud beasts have not trodden it,
Nor hath the fierce lion passed thereby.
He putteth forth his hand upon the flinty rock;
He overturneth the mountains by the roots.
He cutteth out channels among the rocks;
And his eye seeth every precious thing.
He bindeth the streams that they trickle not;
And the thing that is hid bringeth he forth to light.
But where shall wisdom be found?

13

And where is the place of understanding?
Man knoweth not the price thereof;
Neither is it found in the land of the living.
The deep saith, It is not in me:
And the sea saith, It is not with me.
It cannot be gotten for gold,
Neither shall silver be weighed for the price thereof.
It cannot be valued with the gold of Ophir,
With the precious onyx, or the sapphire.
Gold and glass cannot equal it:
Neither shall the exchange thereof be jewels of fine gold.
No mention shall be made of coral or of crystal:
Yea, the price of wisdom is above rubies.
The topaz of Ethiopia shall not equal it,
Neither shall it be valued with pure gold.
Whence then cometh wisdom?
And where is the place of understanding?
Seeing it is hid from the eyes of all living,
And kept close from the fowls of the air.
Destruction and Death say,
We have heard a rumour thereof with our ears.
God understandeth the way thereof,
And he knoweth the place thereof.
For he looketh to the ends of the earth,
And seeth under the whole heaven;
To make a weight for the wind;
Yea, he meteth out the waters by measure.
When he made a decree for the rain,
And a way for the lightning of the thunder:
Then did he see it, and declare it;
He established it, yea, and searched it out.
And unto man he said,
Behold, the fear of the Lord, *that* is wisdom;
And to depart from evil is understanding.

Is that poetry? Surely it is poetry. Can you improve
it with the embellishments of rhyme and strict scansion?

Well, sundry bold men have tried, and I will choose, for your judgment, the rendering of a part of the above passage by one who is by no means the worst of them— a hardy anonymous Scotsman. His version was published at Falkirk in 1869:

> His hand on the rock the adventurer puts,
> And mountains entire overturns by the roots;
> New rivers in rocks are enchased by his might,
> And everything precious revealed to his sight;
> The floods from o'er-flowing he bindeth at will,
> And the thing that is hid bringeth forth by his skill.
>
> But where real wisdom is found can he shew?
> Or the place understanding inhabiteth? No!
> Men know not the value, the price of this gem;
> 'Tis not found in the land of the living with them.
> It is not in me, saith the depth; and the sea
> With the voice of an echo, repeats, Not in me.

(I have a suspicion somehow that what the sea really answered, in its northern vernacular, was "Me either.")

> Whence then cometh wisdom? And where is the place
> Understanding hath chosen, since this is the case? . . .

Enough! This not only shows how that other rendering can be spoilt even to the point of burlesque by an attempt, on preconceived notions, to embellish it with metre and rhyme, but it also hints that parallel verse will actually resent and abhor such embellishment even by the most skilled hand. Yet, I repeat, our version of *Job* is poetry undeniable. What follows?

Why, it follows that in the course of studying it as

literature we have found experimentally settled for us—and on the side of freedom—a dispute in which scores of eminent critics have taken sides: a dispute revived but yesterday (if we omit the blank and devastated days of this War) by the writers and apostles of *vers libres*. "Can there be poetry without metre?" "Is free verse a true poetic form?" Why, our *Book of Job* being poetry, unmistakable poetry, of course there can, to be sure it is. These apostles are butting at an open door. Nothing remains for them but to go and write *vers libres* as fine as those of *Job* in our English translation. Or suppose even that they write as well as M. Paul Fort, they will yet be writing ancestrally, not as innovators but as renewers. Nothing is done in literature by arguing whether or not this or that be possible or permissible. The only way to prove it possible or permissible is to go and do it: and then you are lucky indeed if some ancient writers have not forestalled you.

IV

Now for another question (much argued, you will remember, a few years ago) "Is there—can there be—such a thing as a Static Theatre, a Static Drama?"

Most of you (I daresay) remember M. Maeterlinck's definition of this and his demand for it. To summarise him roughly, he contends that the old drama—the traditional, the conventional drama—lives by action; that, in Aristotle's phrase, it represents men doing πράττοντας and resolves itself into a struggle of human wills—whether against the gods, as in ancient tragedy, or against one another, as in modern.   M. Maeterlinck tells us—

There is a tragic element in the life of every day that is far more real, far more penetrating, far more akin to the true self that is in us, than is the tragedy that lies in great adventure. . . .   It goes beyond the determined struggle of man against man, and desire against desire; it goes beyond the eternal conflict of duty and passion.   Its province is rather to reveal to us how truly wonderful is the mere act of living, and to throw light upon the existence of the soul, self-contained in the midst of ever-restless immensities; to hush the discourse of reason and sentiment, so that above the tumult may be heard the solemn uninterrupted whisperings of man and his destiny.

To the tragic author [he goes on, later], as to the mediocre painter who still lingers over historical pictures, it is only the violence of the anecdote that appeals, and in his representation thereof does the entire interest of his work consist. . . .   Indeed when I go to a theatre, I feel as though I were spending a few hours with my ancestors, who conceived life as though it were something that was primitive, arid and brutal. . . .   I am shown a deceived husband killing his wife, a woman poisoning her lover, a son avenging his father, a father slaughtering his children, murdered kings, ravished virgins, imprisoned citizens—in a word all the sublimity of tradition, but alas how superficial and material!   Blood, surface-tears and death!   What can I learn from creatures who have but one fixed idea, who have no time to live, for that there is a rival, a mistress, whom it behoves them to put to death?

M. Maeterlinck does not (he says) know if the Static Drama of his craving be impossible.   He inclines to think—instancing some Greek tragedies such as *Pro-*

metheus and *Choephori*—that it already exists. But may we not, out of the East—the slow, the stationary East—fetch an instance more convincing?

V

The Drama of Job opens with a *Prologue* in the mouth of a Narrator.

There was a man in the land of Uz, named Job; upright, God-fearing, of great substance in sheep, cattle and oxen; blest also with seven sons and three daughters. After telling of their family life, how wholesome it is, and pious, and happy—

The Prologue passes to a Council held in Heaven. The Lord sits there, and the sons of God present themselves each from his province. Enters Satan (whom we had better call the Adversary) from his sphere of inspection, the Earth, and reports. The Lord specially questions him concerning Job, pattern of men. The Adversary demurs. "Doth Job fear God for nought? Hast thou not set a hedge about his prosperity? But put forth thy hand and touch all that he hath, and he will renounce thee to thy face." The Lord gives leave for this trial to be made (you will recall the opening of *Everyman*):

So, in the midst of his wealth, a messenger came to Job and said—

> The oxen were plowing,
> and the asses feeding beside them:
> and the Sabeans fell upon them,
> and took them away;

yea, they have slain the servants with the edge of the sword;
and I only am escaped alone to tell thee.

While he was yet speaking, there came also another, and
said,
The fire of God is fallen from heaven,
and hath burned up the sheep, and the servants,
and consumed them;
and I only am escaped alone to tell thee.

While he was yet speaking, there came also another, and
said,
The Chaldeans made three bands,
and fell upon the camels,
and have taken them away,
yea, and slain the servants with the edge of the sword;
and I only am escaped alone to tell thee.

While he was yet speaking, there came also another, and
said,
Thy sons and thy daughters
were eating and drinking wine in their eldest brother's
house:
and, behold,
there came a great wind from the wilderness,
and smote the four corners of the house,
and it fell upon the young men,
and they are dead;
and I only am escaped alone to tell thee.

Then Job arose, and rent his mantle, and shaved his head,
and
fell down upon the ground, and worshipped; and he said,
Naked came I out of my mother's womb,
And naked shall I return thither:
The Lord gave, and the Lord hath taken away;
blessed be the name of the Lord.

So the Adversary is foiled, and Job has not renounced God.

A second Council is held in Heaven; and the Adversary, being questioned, has to admit Job's integrity, but proposes a severer test:

Skin for skin, yea, all that a man hath will he give for his life. But put forth thine hand now, and touch his bone and his flesh, and he will renounce thee to thy face.

Again leave is given: and the Adversary smites Job with the most hideous and loathsome form of leprosy. His kinsfolk (as we learn later) have already begun to desert and hold aloof from him as a man marked out by God's displeasure. But now he passes out from their midst, as one unclean from head to foot, and seats himself on the ash-mound—that is, upon the Mezbele or heap of refuse which accumulates outside Arab villages.

"The dung," says Professor Moulton, "which is heaped upon the Mezbele of the Hauran villages is not mixed with straw, which in that warm and dry land is not needed for litter, and it comes mostly from solid-hoofed animals, as the flocks and oxen are left over-night in the grazing places. It is carried in baskets in a dry state to this place . . . and usually burnt once a month. . . . The ashes remain. . . . If the village has been inhabited for centuries the Mezbele reaches a height far overtopping it. The winter rains reduce it into a compact mass, and it becomes by and by a solid hill of earth. . . . The Mezbele serves the inhabitants for a watchtower, and in the sultry evenings for a place of concourse, because there is a current of air on the height. There all day long the children play about it; and

there the outcast, who has been stricken with some loathsome malady, and is not allowed to enter the dwellings of
men, lays himself down, begging an alms of the passers-by
by day, and by night sheltering himself among the ashes
which the heat of the sun has warmed."

Here, then sits in his misery "the forsaken grandee";
and here yet another temptation comes to him—this
time not expressly allowed by the Lord. Much foolish
condemnation (and, I may add, some foolish facetious-
ness) has been heaped on Job's wife. As a matter of
fact she is *not* a wicked woman—she has borne her part
in the pious and happy family life, now taken away: she
has uttered no word of complaint though all the substance be swallowed up and her children with it. But
now the sight of her innocent husband thus helpless,
thus incurably smitten, wrings, through love and
anguish and indignation, this cry from her:

Dost thou still hold fast thine integrity? renounce God,
and die.

But Job answered, soothing her:

Thou speakest as one of the foolish women speaketh.
What? shall we receive good at the hand of God, and shall
we not receive evil?

So the second trial ends, and Job has sinned not with
his lips.
But now comes the third trial, which needs no
Council in Heaven to decree it. Travellers by the
mound saw this figure seated there, patient, uncom-

plaining, an object of awe even to the children who at
first mocked him; asked this man's history; and hearing
of it, smote on their breasts, and made a token of it and
carried the news into far countries: until it reached the
ears of Job's three friends, all great tribesmen like himself—Eliphaz the Temanite, Bildad the Shuhite, and
Zophar the Naamathite. These three made an appoint-
ment together to travel and visit Job. "And when they
lifted up their eyes afar off, and knew him not, they
lifted up their voice and wept." Then they went up and
sat down opposite him on the ground. But the majesty
of suffering is silent:

> Here I and sorrows sit;
> Here is my throne, bid kings come bow to it. . . .

No, not a word. . . . And, with the grave courtesy
of Eastern men, they too are silent:

So they sat down with him upon the ground seven days
and seven nights, and none spake a word unto him: for they
saw that his grief was very great.

The Prologue ends. The scene is set. After seven
days of silence the real drama opens.

VI

Of the drama itself I shall attempt no analysis, referring you for this to the two books from which I have
already quoted. My purpose being merely to persuade
you that this surpassing poem can be studied, and ought
to be studied, as literature, I shall content myself with

turning it (so to speak) once or twice in my hand and glancing one or two facets at you.

To begin with, then, you will not have failed to notice, in the setting out of the drama, a curious resemblance between *Job* and the *Prometheus* of Æschylus. The curtain in each play lifts on a figure solitary, tortured (for no reason that seems good to us) by a higher will which, we are told, is God's. The chorus of Sea-nymphs in the opening of the Greek play bears no small resemblance in attitude of mind to Job's three friends. When Job at length breaks the intolerable silence with

Let the day perish wherein I was born,
And the night which said, There is a man child conceived.

he uses just such an outburst as Prometheus: and, as he is answered by his friends, so the Nymphs at once exclaim to Prometheus

Seest thou not that thou hast sinned?

But at once, for anyone with a sense of comparative literature, is set up a comparison between the persistent West and the persistent East; between the fiery energising rebel and the patient victim. Of these two, both good, one will dare everything to release mankind from thrall; the other will submit, and justify himself—mankind too, if it may hap—by submission.

At once this difference is seen to give a difference of form to the drama. Our poem is purely static. Some critics can detect little individuality in Job's three

friends, to distinguish them. For my part I find Eliphaz
more of a personage than the other two; grander in the
volume of his mind, securer in wisdom; as I find Zophar
rather noticeably a mean-minded greybeard, and Bildad
a man of the stand-no-nonsense kind. But, to tell the
truth, I prefer not to search for individuality in these
men: I prefer to see them as three figures with eyes of
stone almost expressionless. For in truth they are the
conventions, all through,—the orthodox men—addressing Job, the reality; and their words come to this:

> Thou sufferest, therefore must have sinned.
> All suffering is, must be a judgment upon sin.
> Else God is not righteous.

They are statuesque, as the drama is static. The speeches
follow one another, rising and falling, in rise and fall
magnificently and deliberately eloquent. Not a limb is
seen to move, unless it be when Job half rises from the
dust in sudden scorn of their conventions:

> No doubt but *ye* are the people,
> And wisdom shall die with you!

or again

> Will *ye* speak unrighteously for God,
>   And talk deceitfully for him?
> Will *ye* respect *his* person?
> Will *ye* contend for God?

Yet—so great is this man, who has not renounced and
will not renounce God, that still and ever he clamours
for more knowledge of Him. Still getting no answer,
he lifts up his hands and calls the great Oath of Clear-

ance; in effect, If I have loved gold overmuch, hated mine enemy, refused the stranger my tent, truckled to public opinion:

> If my land cry out against me,
>   And the furrows thereof weep together;
> If I have eaten the fruits thereof without money,
> Or have caused the owners thereof to lose their life:
>   Let thistles grow instead of wheat,
>   And cockle instead of barley.

With a slow gesture he covers his face:

> The words of Job are ended.

VII

They are ended: even though at this point (when the debate seems to be closed) a young Aramaean Arab, Elihu, who has been loitering around and listening to the controversy, bursts in and delivers his young red-hot opinions. They are violent, and at the same time quite raw and priggish. Job troubles not to answer: the others keep a chilling silence. But while this young man rants, pointing skyward now and again, we see, we feel—it is most wonderfully conveyed—as clearly as if indicated by successive stage-directions, a terrific thunder-storm gathering; a thunder-storm with a whirlwind. It gathers; it is upon them; it darkens them with dread until even the words of Elihu dry on his lips:

> If a man speak, surely he shall be swallowed up.

It breaks and blasts and confounds them; and out of it the Lord speaks.

Now of that famous and marvellous speech, put by the poet into the mouth of God, we may say what may be said of all speeches put by man into the mouth of God. We may say, as of the speeches of the Archangel in *Paradise Lost* that it is argument, and argument, by its very nature, admits of being answered. But, if to make God talk at all be anthropomorphism, here is anthropomorphism at its very best in its effort to reach to God.

There is a hush. The storm clears away; and in this hush the voice of the Narrator is heard again, pronouncing the Epilogue. Job has looked in the face of God and reproached him as a friend reproaches a friend. Therefore his captivity was turned, and his wealth returned to him, and he begat sons and daughters, and saw his son's sons unto the fourth generation. So Job died, being old and full of years.

VIII

Structurally a great poem; historically a great poem; philosophically a great poem; so rendered for us in noble English diction as to be worthy in any comparison of diction, structure, ancestry, thought! Why should we not study it in our English School, if only for purpose of comparison? I conclude with these words of Lord Latymer:

There is nothing comparable with it except the *Prometheus Bound* of Æschylus. It is eternal, illimitable . . . its scope is the relation between God and Man. It is a vast liberation, a great gaol-delivery of the spirit of Man; nay rather a great Acquittal.

OF SELECTION

I

L ET us hark back, Gentlemen, to our original problem, and consider if our dilatory way have led us to some glimpse of a practical solution.

We may re-state it thus: Assuming it to be true, as men of Science assure us, that the weight of this planet remains constant, and is to-day what it was when mankind carelessly laid it on the shoulders of Atlas; that nothing abides but it goes, that nothing goes but in some form or other it comes back; you and I may well indulge a wonder what reflections upon this astonishing fact our University Librarian, Mr. Jenkinson, takes to bed with him. A copy of every book printed in the United Kingdom is—or I had better say, should be—deposited with him. Putting aside the question of what he has done to deserve it, he must surely wonder at times from what other corners of the earth Providence has been at pains to collect and compact the ingredients of the latest new volume he handles for a moment before fondly committing it to the cellars.

"Locked up, not lost."

Or, to take it in reverse—When the great library of Alexandria went up in flames, doubtless its ashes awoke an appreciable and almost immediate energy in the crops of the Nile Delta. The more leisurable process of desiccation, by which, under modern storage, the components of a modern novel are released to fresh unions and activities admits, as Sir Thomas Browne would say, a wide solution, and was just the question to tease that good man. Can we not hear him discussing it? "To be but pyramidally extant is a fallacy in duration. . . . To burn the bones of the King of Edom for lime seems no irrational ferity: but to store the back volumes of Mr. Bottomley's *John Bull* a passionate prodigality."

II

Well, whatever the perplexities of our Library we may be sure they will never break down that tradition of service, help, and courtesy which is, among its fine treasures, still the first. But we have seen that Mr. Jenkinson's perplexities are really but a parable of ours: that the question, What are we to do with all these books accumulating in the world? really *is* a question: that their mere accumulation really *does* heap up against us a barrier of such enormous and brute mass that the stream of human culture must needs be choked and spread into marsh unless we contrive to pipe it through. That a great deal of it is meant to help—that even the most of it is well intentioned—avails not against the mere physical obstacle of its mass. If you consider an Athenian gentleman of the fourth century B.C. connecting (as I always preach here) his literature with his life, two things are bound to strike you: the first that he was a man of leisure, somewhat disdainful of trade and relieved of menial work by a number of slaves; the second, that he was surprisingly unencumbered with books. You will find in Plato much about reciters, actors, poets, rhetoricians, pleaders, sophists, public orators, and refiners of language, but very little indeed about books. Even the library of Alexandria grew in a time of decadence and belonged to an age not his. Says Jowett in the end:

"He who approaches him in the most reverent spirit shall reap most of the fruit of his wisdom; he who reads him by the light of ancient commentators will have the least understanding of him.

"We see him [Jowett goes on] with the eye of the mind in the groves of the Academy, or on the banks of the Ilissus, or in the streets of Athens, alone or walking with Socrates, full of those thoughts which have since become the common possession of mankind. Or we may compare him to a statue hid away in some temple of Zeus or Apollo, no longer existing on earth, a statue which has a look as of the God himself. Or we may once more imagine him following in another state of being the great company of heaven which he beheld of old in a vision. So," partly trifling but with a certain degree of seriousness, "we linger around the memory of a world which has passed away."

Yes, "which has passed away," and perhaps with no token more evident of its decease that the sepulture of books that admiring generations have heaped on it!

III

In a previous lecture I referred you to the beautiful opening and the yet more beautiful close of the *Phaedrus*.

14

Let us turn back and refresh ourselves with that
Dialogue while we learn from it, in somewhat more of
detail, just what a book meant to an Athenian: how
fresh a thing it was to him and how little irksome.

Phaedrus has spent his forenoon listening to a discourse by the celebrated rhetorician Lysias on the
subject of Love, and is starting to cool his head with a
stroll beyond the walls of the city, when he encounters
Socrates, who will not let him go until he has delivered
up the speech with which Lysias regaled him, or, better
still, the manuscript, "which I suspect you are carrying
there in your left hand under your cloak." So they
bend their way beside Ilissus towards a tall plane tree,
seen in the distance. Having reached it, they recline.

"By Hera," says Socrates, "a fair resting-place, full of
summer sounds and scents! This clearing, with the *agnus
castus* in high bloom and fragrant, and the stream beneath
the tree so gratefully cool to our feet! Judging from the
ornaments and statues, I think this spot must be sacred to
Acheloüs and the Nymphs. And the breeze, how deliciously
charged with balm! and all summer's murmur in the air,
shrilled by the chorus of the grasshoppers! But the greatest
charm is this knoll of turf,—positively a pillow for the head.
My dear Phaedrus, you have been a delectable guide."

"What an incomprehensible being you are, Socrates,"
returns Phaedrus. "When you are in the country, as you
say, you really are like some stranger led about by a guide.
Upon my word, I doubt if you ever stray beyond the gates
save by accident."

"Very true, my friend: and I hope you will forgive me for
the reason—which is, that I love knowledge, and my
teachers are the men who dwell in the city, not the trees or
country scenes. Yet I do believe you have found a spell to

draw me forth, like a hungry cow before whom a bough or a
bunch of fruit is waved. For only hold up before me in like
manner a book, and you may lead me all round Attica and
over the wide world."

So they recline and talk, looking aloft through that
famous pure sky of Attica, mile upon mile transparent;
and their discourse (preserved to us) is of Love, and
seems to belong to that atmosphere, so clear it is and
luminously profound. It ends with the cool of the day,
and the two friends arise to depart. Socrates looks
about him.

"Should we not before going, offer up a prayer to
these local deities?"

"By all means," Phaedrus agrees.

Socrates (praying): "Beloved Pan, and all ye other gods
who haunt this place, grant me beauty in the inward soul,
and that the outward and inward may be at one! May I
esteem the wise to be the rich; and may I myself have that
quantity of gold which a temperate man, and he only, can
carry. . . . Anything more? That prayer, I think, is
enough for me."
Phaedrus. "Ask the same for me, Socrates. Friends,
methinks should have all things in common."
Socrates. "So be it. . . . Let us go."

Here we have, as it seems to me, a marriage, without
impediment, of wisdom and beauty between two minds
that perforce have small acquaintance with books: and
yet, with it, Socrates' confession that anyone with a
book under his cloak could lead him anywhere by the
nose. So we see that Hellenic culture at its best was
independent of book-learning, and yet craved for it.

IV

When our own Literature awoke, taking its origin from the proud scholarship of the Renaissance, an Englishman who affected it was scarcely more cumbered with books than our Athenian had been, two thousand years before. It was, and it remained, aristocratic: sparingly expensive of its culture. It postulated, if not a slave population, at least a proletariat for which its blessings were not. No one thought of making a fortune by disseminating his work in print. Shakespeare never found it worth while to collect and publish his plays; and a very small sense of history will suffice to check our tears over the price received by Milton for *Paradise Lost*. We may wonder, indeed, at the time it took our forefathers to realise—or, at any rate, to employ—the energy that lay in the printing-press. For centuries after its invention mere copying commanded far higher prices than authorship.[1] Writers gave "authorised" editions to the world sometimes for the sake of fame, often to justify themselves against piratical publishers, seldom in expectation of monetary profit. Listen, for example, to Sir Thomas Browne's excuse for publishing *Religio Medici* (1643):

Had not almost every man suffered by the press or were not the tyranny thereof become universal, I had not wanted reason for complaint: but in times wherein I have lived to behold the highest perversion of that excellent invention, the name of his Majesty defamed, the honour of Parliament depraved, the writings of both depravedly, anticipatively,

[1] Charles Reade notes this in *The Cloister and the Hearth*, Chap. LXI.

counterfeitly imprinted; complaints may seem ridiculous
in private persons; and men of my condition may be as in-
capable of affronts, as hopeless of their reparations. And
truly had not the duty I owe unto the importunity of
friends, and the allegiance I must ever acknowledge unto
truth, prevailed with me; the inactivity of my disposition
might have made these sufferings continual, and time that
brings other things to light, should have satisfied me in the
remedy of its oblivion. But because things evidently false
are not only printed, but many things of truth most falsely
set forth, in this latter I could not but think myself engaged.
For though we have no power to redress the former, yet in
the other, the reparation being within ourselves, I have at
present represented unto the world a full and intended copy
of that piece, which was most imperfectly and surrepti-
tiously published before.

This I confess, about seven years past, with some others
of affinity thereto, for my private exercise and satisfaction,
I had at leisurable hours composed; which being communicated unto one, it became common unto many, and was by
transcription successively corrupted, until it arrived in a
most depraved copy at the press. . . . [1]

V

The men of the eighteenth century maintained the old
tradition of literary exclusiveness, but in a somewhat
different way and more consciously.

I find, Gentlemen, when you read with me in private,
that nine out of ten of you dislike the eighteenth century and all its literary works. As for the women

---

[1] The loose and tautologous style of this Preface is worth noting.
Likely enough Browne wrote it in a passion that deprived him of his
habitual self-command. One phrase alone reveals the true Browne—
that is, Browne true to himself: "and time that brings other things to
light, should have satisfied me in the remedy of its oblivion."

students, they one and all abominate it. You do not, I regret to say, provide me with reasons much more philosophical than the epigrammatist's for disliking Doctor Fell. May one whose time of life excuses perhaps a detachment from passion attempt to provide you with one? If so, first listen to this from Mr. and Mrs. Hammond's book *The Village Labourer*, 1760–1832:

A row of eighteenth century houses, or a room of normal eighteenth century furniture, or a characteristic piece of eighteenth century literature, conveys at once a sensation of satisfaction and completeness. The secret of this charm is not to be found in any special beauty or nobility of design or expression, but simply in an exquisite fitness. The eighteenth century mind was a unity, an order. All literature and art that really belong to the eighteenth century are the language of a little society of men and women who moved within one set of ideas; who understood each other; who were not tormented by any anxious or bewildering problems; who lived in comfort, and, above all things, in composure. The classics were their freemasonry. There was a standard for the mind, for the emotions, for taste: there were no incongruities.

When you have a society like this, you have what we roughly call a civilisation, and it leaves its character and canons in all its surroundings and in its literature. Its definite ideas lend themselves readily to expression. A larger society seems an anarchy in contrast; just because of its escape into a greater world it seems powerless to stamp itself in wood or stone; it is condemned as an age of chaos and mutiny, with nothing to declare.

You do wrong, I assure you, in misprising these men of the eighteenth century. They reduced life, to be sure: but by that very means they saw it far more

completely than do we, in this lyrical age with our worship of "fine excess." Here at any rate, and to speak
only of its literature, you have a society fencing that
literature around—I do not say by forethought or even
consciously—but in effect fencing its literature around,
to keep it in control and capable of an orderly, a nice,
even an exquisite cultivation. Dislike it as you may, I
do not think that any of you, as he increases his knowledge of the technique of English Prose, yes, and of
English Verse (I do not say of English Poetry) will deny
his admiration to the men of the eighteenth century.
The strength of good prose resides not so much in the
swing and balance of the single sentence as in the marshalling of argument, the orderly procession of paragraphs, the disposition of parts so that each finds its
telling, its proper place; the adjustment of the means
to the end; the strategy which brings its full force into
action at the calculated moment and drives the conclusion home upon an accumulated sense of *justice*. I
do not see how any student of eighteenth century literature can deny its writers—Berkeley or Hume or Gibbon
—Congreve or Sheridan—Pope or Cowper—Addison or
Steele or Johnson—Burke or Chatham or Thomas
Payne—their meed for this, or, if he be an artist, even
his homage.

But it remains true, as your instinct tells you, and as
I have admitted, that they achieved all this by help of
narrow and artificial boundaries. Of several fatal ex-
clusions let me name but two.

In the first place, they excluded the Poor; imitating

in a late age the Athenian tradition of a small polite
society resting on a large and degraded one. Throughout the eighteenth century—and the great Whig families
were at least as much to blame for this as the Tories—
by enclosure of commons, by grants, by handling of the
franchise, by taxation, by poor laws in result punitive
though intended to be palliative, the English peasantry
underwent a steady process of degradation into serfdom;
into a serfdom which, during the first twenty years of
the next century, hung constantly and precariously on
the edge of actual starvation. The whole theory of
culture worked upon a principle of double restriction;
of restricting on the one hand the realm of polite
knowledge to propositions suitable for a scholar and
a gentleman: and, on the other, the numbers of the
human family permitted to be either. The theory
deprecated enthusiasm, as it discountenanced all ambition in a poor child to rise above what Sir Spencer
Walpole called "his inevitable and hereditary lot"—
to soften which and make him acquiescent in it was,
with a Wilberforce or a Hannah More, the last dream
of restless benevolence.

VI

Also these eighteenth century men fenced off the
whole of our own Middle English and mediæval literature—fenced off Chaucer and Dunbar, Malory and
Berners—as barbarous and "Gothic." They treated
these writers with little more consideration than Boileau

had thought it worth while to bestow on Villon or on
Ronsard—*enfin Malherbe!* As for Anglo-Saxon literature, one may safely say that, save by Gray and a very
few others, its existence was barely surmised.

You may or may not find it harder to forgive them
that they ruled out moreover a great part of the literature of the preceding century as offensive to urbane
taste or as they would say, "disgusting." They disliked
it mainly, one suspects, as one age revolts from the
fashion of another—as some of you, for example, revolt
from the broad plenty of Dickens (Heaven forgive you)
or the ornament of Tennyson. Some of the great
writers of that age definitely excluded God from their
scheme of things: others included God fiercely, but with
circumscription and limitation. I think it fair to say of
them generally that they hated alike the mystical and
the mysterious, and, hating these, could have little
commerce with such poetry as Crashaw's and Vaughan's
or such speculation as gave ardour to the prose of the
Cambridge Platonists. Johnson's famous attack, in his
Life of Cowley, upon the metaphysical followers of
Donne ostensibly assails their literary conceits, but
truly and at bottom rests its quarrel against an attitude
of mind, in respect of which he lived far enough removed
to be unsympathetic yet near enough to take denuncia-
tion for a duty. Johnson, to put it vulgarly, had as
little use for Vaughan's notion of poetry as he would
have had for Shelley's claim that it

> feeds on the aëreal kisses
> Of shapes that haunt thought's wildernesses,

and we have only to set ourselves back in Shelley's age and read (say) the verse of Frere and Canning in *The Anti-Jacobin*, to understand how frantic a lyrist—let be how frantic a political figure—Shelley must have appeared to well regulated minds.

VII

All this literature which our forefathers excluded has come back upon us: and concurrently we have to deal with the more serious difficulty (let us give thanks for it) of a multitude of millions insurgent to handsel their long-deferred heritage. I shall waste no time in arguing that we ought not to wish to withhold it, because we cannot if we would. And thus the problem becomes a double one, of *distribution* as well as of *selection*.

Now in the first place I submit that this *distribution* should be free: which implies that our *selection* must be confined to books and methods of teaching. There must be no picking and choosing among the recipients, no appropriation of certain forms of culture to certain "stations of life" with a tendency, conscious or unconscious, to keep those stations as stationary as possible.

Merely by clearing our purpose to this extent we shall have made no inconsiderable advance. For even the last century never quite got rid of its predecessor's fixed idea that certain degrees of culture were appropriate to certain stations of life. With what gentle persistence it prevails, for example, in Jane Austen's novels; with what complacent rhetoric in Tennyson (and in spite of

Lady Clara Vere de Vere)! Let me remind you that by
allowing an idea to take hold of our animosity we may
be as truly "possessed" by it as though it claimed our
allegiance. The notion that culture may be drilled to
march in step with a trade or calling endured through
the Victorian age of competition and possessed the mind
not only of Samuel Smiles who taught by instances how
a bright and industrious boy might earn money and
lift himself out of his "station," but of Ruskin himself,
who in the first half of *Sesame and Lilies*, in the lecture
Of King's Treasuries, discussing the choice of books,
starts vehemently and proceeds at length to denounce
the prevalent passion for self-advancement—of rising
above one's station in life—quite as if it were the most
important thing, willy-nilly, in talking of the choice of
books. Which means that, to Ruskin, just then, it
was the most formidable obstacle. Can we, at this time
of day, do better by simply turning the notion out of
doors? Yes, I believe that we can: and upon this *credo:*

*I believe that while it may grow—and grow infinitely—
with increase of learning, the grace of a liberal education,
like the grace of Christianity, is so catholic a thing—so
absolutely above being trafficked, retailed, apportioned,
among "stations in life"—that the humblest child may
claim it by indefensible right, having a soul.*

*Further, I believe that Humanism is, or should be, no
decorative appanage, purchased late in the process of education within the means of a few: but a quality, rather, which
should, and can, condition all teaching, from a child's first
lesson in Reading: that its unmistakable hall-mark can be*

*impressed upon the earliest task set in an Elementary
School.*

VIII

I am not preaching red Radicalism in this: I am not
telling you that Jack is as good as his master: if he were,
he would be a great deal better; for he would understand Homer (say) as well as his master, the child of
parents who could afford to have him taught Greek.
As Greek is commonly taught, I regret to say, whether
they have learnt it or not makes a distressingly small
difference to most boys' appreciation of Homer. Still
it does make a vast difference to some, and should make
a vast difference to all. And yet, if you will read the
passage in Kinglake's *Eöthen* in which he tells—in words
that find their echo in many a reader's memory—of his
boyish passion for Homer—and if you will note that the
boy imbibed his passion, after all, through the conduit
of Pope's translation—you will acknowledge that, for
the human boy, admission to much of the glory of
Homer's realm does not depend upon such mastery as a
boy of fifteen or sixteen possesses over the original. But
let me quote you a few sentences:

I, too, loved Homer, but not with a scholar's love. The
most humble and pious among women was yet so proud a
mother that she could teach her first-born son no Watts's
hymns, no collects for the day; she could teach him in earliest childhood no less than this—to find a home in his saddle,
and to love old Homer, and all that old Homer sung. True, it
is, that the Greek was ingeniously rendered into English,

the English of Pope even, but not even a mesh like that can screen an earnest child from the fire of Homer's battles.

I pored over the *Odyssey* as over a story-book, hoping and fearing for the hero whom yet I partly scorned. But the *Iliad*—line by line I clasped it to my brain with reverence as well as with love. . . .

The impatient child is not grubbing for beauties, but pushing the siege; the women vex him with their delays, and their talking, . . . but all the while that he thus chafes at the pausing of the action, the strong vertical light of Homer's poetry is blazing so full upon the people and things of the *Iliad*, that soon to the eyes of the child they grow familiar as his mother's shawl. . . .

It was not the recollection of school nor college learning, but the rapturous and earnest reading of my childhood, which made me bend forward so longingly to the plains of Troy.

IX

It is among the books then, and not among the readers, that we must do our selecting. But how? On what principle or principles?

Sometime in the days of my youth, a newspaper, *The Pall Mall Gazette*, then conducted by W. T. Stead, made a conscious effort to solve the riddle by inviting a number of eminent men to compile lists of the Hundred Best Books. Now this invitation rested on a fallacy. Considering for a moment how personal a thing is Literature, you will promptly assure yourselves that there is—there can be—no such thing as the Hundred Best Books. If you yet incline to toy with the notion, carry it on and compile a list of the Hundred Second-best Books: nay, if you will, continue until you find yourself solemnly, with a brow corrugated by responsibility, weighing the claims (say) of Velleius Paterculus, Paul and Virginia and Mr. Jorrocks to admission among the Hundred Tenth-best Books. There is in fact no positive hierarchy among the classics. You cannot appraise the worth of Charles Lamb against the worth of Casaubon: the worth of Hesiod against the worth of Madame de Sévigné: the worth of Théophile Gautier against the worth of Dante or Thomas Hobbes or Macchiavelli or Jane Austen. They all wrote with pens, in ink, upon paper: but you no sooner pass beyond these resemblances than your comparison finds itself working in *impari materia*.

Also why should the Best Books be 100 in number, rather than 99 or 199? And under what conditions is a book a Best Book? There are moods in which we not only prefer Pickwick to the Rig-Vedas or Sakuntalà, but find that it does us more good. In our day again I pay all respect to Messrs. Dent's *Everyman's Library*. It was a large conception carefully planned. But, in the nature of things, Everyman is going to arrive at a point beyond which he will find it more and more difficult to recognise himself: at a point, let us say, when Everyman, opening a new parcel, starts to doubt if, after all, it wouldn't be money in his pocket to be Somebody Else.

X

And yet, may be, *The Pall Mall Gazette* was on the right scent. For it was in search of masterpieces: and, however we teach, our trust will in the end repose upon masterpieces, upon the great classics of whatever Language or Literature we are handling: and these, in any language are neither enormous in number and mass, nor extraordinarily difficult to detect, nor (best of all) forbidding to the reader by reason of their own difficulty. Upon a selected few of these—even upon three, or two, or one—we may teach at least a surmise of the true delight, and may be some measure of taste whereby our pupil will, by an inner guide, be warned to choose the better and reject the worse when we turn him loose to read for himself.

To this use of masterpieces I shall devote my final lecture.

ON THE USE OF MASTERPIECES

I

I DO not think, Gentlemen, that we need to bother ourselves to-day with any definition of a "classic," or of the *stigmata* by which a true classic can be recognised. Sainte-Beuve once indicated these in a famous discourse, *Qu'est-ce qu'un classique:* and it may suffice us that these include Universality and Permanence. Your true classic is *universal*, in that it appeals to the catholic mind of man. It is doubly *permanent:* for it remains significant, or acquires a new significance, after the age for which it was written, and the conditions under which it was written have passed away; and it yet keeps, undefaced by handling, the original noble imprint of the mind that first minted it—or shall we say that, as generation after generation rings the coin, it ever returns the echo of its father-spirit?

But for our purpose it suffices that in our literature we possess a number of works to which the title of classic cannot be refused. So let us confine ourselves to these, and to the question, How to use them?

II

Well, to begin with, I revert to a point which I tried to establish in my first lecture; and insist with all my

strength that the first obligation we owe to any classic,
and to those whom we teach, and to ourselves, is to
treat it *absolutely:* not for any secondary or derivative
purpose, or purpose recommended as useful by any
manual: but at first solely to interpret the meaning
which its author intended: that in short we should *trust*
any given masterpiece for its operation, on ourselves
and on others. In that first lecture I quoted to you this
most wise sentence:

That all spirit is mutually attractive, as all matter is ultimately attractive, is an ultimate fact,

and consenting to this with all my heart I say that it
matters very little for the moment, or even for a considerable while, that a pupil does not perfectly, or even
nearly, understand all he reads, provided we can get the
attraction to seize upon him. He and the author
between them will do the rest: our function is to com-
municate and trust. In what other way do children take
the ineffaceable stamp of a gentle nurture than by daily
attraction to whatsoever is beautiful and amiable and
dignified in their home? As there, so in their reading,
the process must be gradual of acquiring an inbred
monitor to reject the evil and choose the good. For it
is the property of masterpieces that they not only raise
you to

despise low Joys, low Gains;
Disdain whatever Cornbury disdains:

they are not only as Lamb wrote of the Plays of Shakespeare "enrichers of the fancy, strengtheners of virtue,

15

a withdrawing from all selfish and mercenary thoughts, a lesson of all sweet and honourable thoughts and actions, to teach you courtesy, benignity, generosity, humanity"; but they raise your gorge to defend you from swallowing the fifth-rate, the sham, the fraudulent. *Abeunt studia in mores.* I cannot, for my part conceive a man who has once incorporated the *Phaedo* or the *Paradiso* or *Lear* in himself as lending himself for a moment to one or other of the follies plastered in these late stern times upon the firm and most solid purpose of this nation—the inanities, let us say, of a Baby-Week. Or, for a more damnable instance, I think of you and me with Marvell's great Horatian Ode sunk in our minds, standing to-day by the statue of Charles I that looks down Whitehall: telling ourselves of "that memorable scene" before the Banqueting House, remembering amid old woes all the glory of our blood and state, recollecting what is due even to ourselves, standing on the greatest site of our capital, and turning to see it degraded as it has been for a week, to a vulgar raree-show. Gentlemen, I could read you many poor ill-written letters from mothers whose sons have died for England, to prove to you we have not deserved *that*, or the sort of placard with which London has been plastered,

Dum domus Aeneae Capitoli immobile saxum
Accolet.

Great enterprises (as we know) and little minds go ill together. Someone veiled the statue. That, at least, was well done.

I have not the information—nor do I want it—to make even a guess who was responsible for this particular outrage. I know the sort of man well enough to venture that he never had a liberal education, and, further, that he is probably rather proud of it. But he may nevertheless own some instinct of primitive kindliness: and I wish he could know how he afflicts men of sensitiveness who have sons at the War.

III

Secondly, let us consider what use we can make of even one selected classic. I refer you back to the work of an old schoolmaster, quoted in my first lecture:

> I believe, if the truth were known, men would be astonished at the small amount of learning with which a high degree of culture is compatible. In a moment of enthusiasm I ventured once to tell my "English set" that if they could really master the ninth book of *Paradise Lost*, so as to rise to the height of its great argument and incorporate all its beauties in themselves, they would at one blow, by virtue of that alone, become highly cultivated men. . . . More and more various learning might raise them to the same height by different paths, but could hardly raise them higher.

I beg your attention for the exact words: "to rise to the height of its great argument and *incorporate all its beauties in themselves*." There you have it—"to incorporate." Do you remember that saying of Wordsworth's, casually dropped in conversation, but preserved for us by Hazlitt?—"It is in the highest degree unphilosophic to call language or diction the dress of our thoughts. . . . It is the *incarnation* of our thoughts." Even so, I maintain to you, the first business of a learner in literature is to get complete hold of some undeniable masterpiece and incorporate it, incarnate it. And, I repeat, there are a few great works for you to choose from: works approved for you by ancient and catholic judgment.

IV

But let us take something far simpler than the Ninth Book of *Paradise Lost* and more direct than any translated masterpiece can be in its appeal; something of high genius, written in our mother tongue. Let us take *The Tempest*.

Of *The Tempest* we may say confidently:

(1) that it is a literary masterpiece: the last most perfect "fruit of the noblest tree in our English Forest";

(2) that its story is quite simple; intelligible to a child: (its basis in fact is fairy-tale, pure and simple— as I tried to show in a previous lecture);

(3) that in reading it—or in reading *Hamlet*, for that matter—the child has no sense at all of being patronised, of being "written down to." And this has the strongest bearing on my argument. The great authors, as Emerson says, never condescend. Shakespeare himself speaks to a slip of a boy, and that boy feels that he *is* Ferdinand;

(4) that, though Shakespeare uses his loftiest, most

accomplished and, in a sense, his most difficult language: a way of talking it has cost him a life-time to
acquire, in line upon line inviting the scholar's, pro-
sodist's, poet's most careful study; that language is no
bar to the child's enjoyment: but rather casts about the
whole play an aura of magnificence which, with the
assistant harmonies, doubles and redoubles the spell.
A child no more resents this because it is strange than he
objects to read in a fairy-tale of robbers concealed in oil-
jars or of diamonds big as a roc's egg. When will our
educators see that what a child depends on is imagination, that what he demands of life is the wonderful, the
glittering, possibility?

Now if, putting all this together and taking confidence from it, we boldly launch a child upon *The
Tempest* we shall come sooner or later upon passages
that *we* have arrived at finding difficult. We shall come,
for example, to the Masque of Iris, which Iris, invoking
Ceres, thus opens:

Ceres, most bounteous lady, thy rich leas
Of wheat, rye, barley, vetches, oats and pease;
Thy turfy mountains, where live nibbling sheep,
And flat meads thatch'd with stover, them to keep;
Thy banks with pionèd and twillèd brims,
Which spongy April at thy hest betrims
To make cold nymphs chaste crowns; and thy broom groves
Whose shadow the dismissèd bachelor loves,
Being lass-lorn; thy pole-clipt vineyard;
And thy sea-marge, sterile and rocky hard
Where thou thyself dost air; the Queen o' the sky
Whose watery arch and messenger am I,
Bids thee leave these. . . .

The passage is undeniably hard for any child, even when you have paused to explain who Ceres is, who Iris, who the Queen o' the sky, and what Iris means by calling herself "her watery arch and messenger." The grammatical structure not only stands on its head but maintains that posture for an extravagant while. Naturally (or rather let us say, ordinarily) it would run, "Ceres, the Queen o' the sky bids thee leave—thy rich leas, etc." But, the lines being twelve-and-a-half in number, we get no hint of there being any grammatical subject until it bursts on us in the second half of line eleven, while the two main verbs and the object of one of them yet linger to be exploded in the last half-line, "Bids thee leave these." · And this again is as nothing to the difficulties of interpretation. "Dismissèd bachelor" may be easy; "pole-clipt vineyard" is certainly not, at first sight. "To make cold nymphs chaste crowns." *What* cold nymphs? You have to wait for another fifty odd lines before being quite sure that Shakespeare means Naiads (and "What are Naiads?" says the child) —"temperate nymphs":

> You nymphs, called Naiades, of the wandering brooks
> With your sedg'd crowns

—and if the child demand what is meant by "pionèd and twillèd brims," you have to answer him that nobody knows.

These difficulties—perhaps for you, certainly for the young reader or listener—are *reserved* delights. My old schoolmaster even indulges this suspicion—"I

never can persuade myself that Shakespeare would have
passed high in a Civil Service Examination on one of his
own plays." At any rate you don't *begin* with these
difficulties: you don't (or I hope you don't) read the
notes first: since, as Bacon puts it, "Studies teach not
their own use."

As for the child, he is not "*grubbing* for beauties";
he magnificently ignores what he cannot for the moment
understand, being intent on *What Is*, the heart and
secret of the adventure. He *is* Ferdinand (I repeat) and
the isle is "full of voices." If these voices were all intelligible, why, then, as Browning would say, "the less
Island it."

V

I have purposely exhibited *The Tempest* at its least
tractable. Who will deny that *as a whole* it can be made
intelligible even to very young children by the simple
process of reading it with them intelligently? or that the
mysteries such a reading leaves unexplained are of the
sort to fascinate a child's mind and allure it? But if this
be granted, I have established my contention that the
Humanities should not be treated as a mere crown and
ornament of education; that they should inform every
part of it, from the beginning, in every school of the
realm: that whether a child have more education or less
education, what he has can be, and should be a "liberal
education" throughout.

Matthew Arnold, as everyone knows, used to preach

the use of these masterpieces as prophylactics of taste.
I would I could make you feel that they are even more
necessary to us.

The reason why?—The reason is that every child
born in these Islands is born into a democracy which,
apart from home affairs, stands committed to a high
responsibility for the future welfare and good gover-
nance of Europe. For three centuries or so it has held
rule over vast stretches of the earth's surface and many
millions of strange peoples: while its obligations
towards the general civilisation of Europe, if not inter-
mittent, have been tightened or relaxed, now here, now
there, by policy, by commerce, by dynastic alliances, by
sudden revulsions or sympathies. But this War will
leave us bound to Europe as we never have been: and,
whether we like it or not, no less inextricably bound to
foe than to friend. Therefore, I say, it has become
important, and in a far higher degree than it ever was
before the War, that our countrymen grow up with a
sense of what I may call the *soul* of Europe. And
nowhere but in literature (which is "memorable
speech")—or at any rate, nowhere so well as in literature—can they find this sense.

VI

There was, as we have seen, a time in Europe, ex-
tending over many centuries, when mankind dwelt
under the preoccupation of making literature, and still
making more of it. The fourth century B.C. in Athens

was such a time; and if you will you may envy, as we all admire, the men of an age when to write at all was tantamount to asserting genius; the men who, in Newman's words, "deserve to be Classics, both because of what they do and because they can do it." If you envy—while you envy—at least remember that these things often paid their price; that the *Phaedo*, for example, was bought for us by the death of Socrates.   Pass Athens and come to Alexandria: still men are accumulating books and the material for books; threshing out the classics into commentaries and grammars, garnering books in great libraries.

There follows an age which interrupts this hive-like labour with sudden and insensate destruction. German tribes from the north, Turkish from the east, break in upon the granaries and send up literature in flames; the Christian Fathers from Tertullian to Gregory the Great (I regret to say) either heartily assisting or at least warming their benedictory hands at the blaze: and so thoroughly they do their work that even the writings of Aristotle, the Philosopher, must wait for centuries as "things silently gone out of mind or things violently destroyed" (to borrow Wordsworth's fine phrase) and creep back into Europe bit by bit, under cover of Arabic translations.

The scholars set to work and begin rebuilding: patient, indefatigable, anonymous as the coral insects at work on a Pacific atoll—building, building, until on the near side of the gulf we call the Dark Age, islets of scholarship lift themselves above the waters: mere specks at first, but ridges appear and connect them: and, to first seeming, sterile enough:

Nec Cereri opportuna seges, nec commoda Baccho—

but as they join and become a *terra firma*, a thin soil gathers on them God knows whence: and, God knows whence, the seed is brought, "it may chance of wheat, or of some other grain." There is a price, again, for this resurrection: but how nobly, how blithely paid you may learn, without seeking recondite examples, from Cuthbert's famous letter describing the death of Bede. Compare that story with that of the last conversation of Socrates; and you will surely recognise that the two men are brothers born out of time; that Bede's work has been a legacy; that his life has been given to re-creating—not scholarship merely nor literature merely —but, through them both, something above them both—the soul of Europe. And this may or may not lead you on to reflect that beyond our present passions, and beyond this War, in a common sanity Europe (and America with her) will have to discover that common soul again.

But eminent spirits such as Bede's are, by their very eminence, less representative of the process—essentially fugitive and self-abnegatory—than the thousands of copyists who have left no name behind them. Let me read you a short paragraph from *The Cambridge History of English Literature*, Chapter II, written, the other day, by one of our own teachers:

The cloister was the centre of life in the monastery, and in the cloister was the workshop of the patient scribe. It is hard to realise that the fair and seemly handwriting of these manuscripts was executed by fingers which, on winter days, when the wind howled through the cloisters, must have been numbed by icy cold. It is true that, occasionally, little carrels or studies in the recesses of the windows were screened off from the main walk of the cloister, and, sometimes, a small room or cell would be partitioned off for the use of a single scribe. The room would then be called the Scriptorium, but it is unlikely that any save the oldest and most learned of the community were afforded this luxury. In these scriptoria of various kinds the earliest annals and chronicles in the English language were penned, in the beautiful and painstaking forms in which we know them.

If you seek testimony, here are the *ipsissima verba* of a poor monk of Wessobrunn endorsed upon his MS:

The book which you now see was written in the outer seats of the cloister. While I wrote I froze: and what I could not write by the beams of day I finished by candle-light.

We might profitably spend—but to-day cannot spare —a while upon the pains these men of the Middle Ages took to accumulate books and to keep them. The chained volumes in old libraries, for example, might give us a text for this as well as start us speculating why it is that, to this day, the human conscience incurably declines to include books with other portable property covered by the Eighth Commandment. Or we might follow several of the early scholars and humanists in

their passionate chasings across Europe, in and out of
obscure monasteries, to recover the lost MSS. of the
classics: might tell, for instance, of Pope Nicholas V,
whose birth-name was Tommaso Parentucelli, and how
he rescued the MSS. from Constantinople and founded
the Vatican Library: or of Aurispa of Sicily who collected two hundred and thirty-eight for Florence: or the
story of the *editio princeps* of the Greek text of Homer.
Or we might dwell on the awaking of our literature,
and the trend given to it, by men of the Italian and
French renaissance; or on the residence of Erasmus
here, in this University, with its results.

VII

But I have said enough to make it clear that, as we
owe so much of our best to understanding Europe, so
the need to understand Europe lies urgently to-day upon
large classes in this country; and that yet, in the nature
of things, these classes can never enjoy such leisure as
our forefathers enjoyed to understand what I call the
soul of Europe, or at least to misunderstand it *upon
acquaintance.*

Let me point out further that within the last few
months we have doubled the difficulty at a stroke by
sharing the government of our country with women and
admitting them to Parliament. It beseems a great
nation to take great risks: to dare them is at once a sign
and a property of greatness: and for good or ill—but for
limitless good as we trust—our country has quietly

made this enterprise amid the preoccupations of the greatest War in its annals. Look at it as you will—let other generations judge it as they will—it stands a monument of our faith in free self-government that in these most perilous days we gave and took so high a guerdon of trust in one another.

But clearly it implies that all the women of this country, down to the small girls entering our elementary schools, must be taught a great many things their mothers and grandmothers—happy in their generation —were content not to know.[1]

It cannot be denied, I think, that in the long course of this War, now [November, 1918] happily on the point of a victorious conclusion, we have suffered heavily through past neglect and present nescience of our literature, which

[1] "Well! . . . my education is at last finished: indeed it would be strange, if, after five years' hard application, anything were left incomplete. Happily that is all over now; and I have nothing to do, but to exercise my various accomplishments.

"Let me see!—as to French, I am mistress of that, and speak it, if possible, with more fluency than English. Italian I can read with ease, and pronounce very well: as well at least, and better, than any of my friends; and that is all one need wish for in Italian. Music I have learned till I am perfectly sick of it. But . . . it will be delightful to play when we have company. I must still continue to practise a little;— the only thing, I think, that I need now to improve myself in. And then there are my Italian songs! which everybody allows I sing with taste, and as it is what so few people can pretend to, I am particularly glad that I can.

"My drawings are universally admired; especially the shells and flowers; which are beautiful, certainly; besides this, I have a decided taste in all kinds of fancy ornaments.

"And then my dancing and waltzing! in which our master himself owned that he could take me no further!—just the figure for it certainly; it would be unpardonable if I did not excel.

"As to common things, geography, and history, and poetry, and philosophy, thank my stars, I have got through them all! so that I may

is so much more European, so much more catholic, a
thing than either our political or our national religion:
that largely by reason of this neglect and this nescience
our statesmen have again and again failed to foresee how
continental nations would act through failing to understand their minds; and have almost invariably, through
this lack of sympathetic understanding, failed to interpret us to foreign friend or foe, even when (and it was
not often) they interpreted us to ourselves. I note that
America—a country with no comparable separate
tradition of literature—has customarily chosen men
distinguished by the grace of letters for ambassadors
to the Court of St. James—Motley, Lowell, Hay, Page,
in our time: and has for her President a man of letters—
and a Professor at that!—whereas, even in these critical
days, Great Britain, having a most noble cause and
at least half-a-hundred writers and speakers capable
of presenting it with dignity and so clearly that no
neutral nation could mistake its logic, has by preference
entrusted it to stunt journalists and film-artistes. If in
these later days you have lacked a voice to interpret
you in the great accent of a Chatham, the cause lies in
past indifference to that literary tradition which is by no
means the least among the glories of our birth and state.

---

consider myself not only perfectly accomplished, but also thoroughly
well-informed.

"Well, to be sure, how much have I fagged through—; the only
wonder is that one head can contain it all."

I found this in a little book *Thoughts of Divines and Philosophers*,
selected by Basil Montagu. The quotation is signed "J. T." I cannot
trace it, but suspect Jane Taylor.

VIII

Masterpieces, then, will serve us as prophylactics of taste, even from childhood; and will help us, further, to interpret the common mind of civilisation. But they have a third and yet nobler use. They teach us to lift our own souls.

For witness to this and to the way of it I am going to call an old writer for whom, be it whim or not, I have an almost eighteenth century reverence—Longinus. No one exactly knows who he was; although it is usual to identify him with that Longinus who philosophised in the court of the Queen Zenobia and was by her, in her downfall, handed over with her other counsellors to be executed by Aurelian: though again, as is usual, certain bold bad men affirm that, whether he was this Longinus or not, the treatise of which I speak was not written by any Longinus at all but by someone with a different name, with which they are unacquainted. Be this as it may, *somebody* wrote the treatise and its first editor, Francis Robertello of Basle, in 1554 called him Dionysius Longinus; and so shall I, and have done with it, careless that other MSS. than that used by Robertello, speak of Dionysius *or* Longinus. Dionysius Longinus, then, in the third century B.C.—some say in the first: it is no great matter—wrote a little book ΠΕΡΙ ΎΨΟΥΣ commonly cited as *Longinus on the Sublime*. The title is handy, but quite misleading, unless you remember that by "Sublimity" Longinus meant, as he expressly defines it, "a certain distinction and excellence in

speech." The book, thus recovered, had great authority
with critics of the seventeenth and eighteenth centuries.
For the last hundred years it has quite undeservedly
gone out of vogue.

It is (I admit) a puzzling book, though quite clear
in argument and language: pellucidly clear, but here
and there strangely modern, even hauntingly modern, if
the phrase may be allowed. You find yourself rubbing
your eyes over a passage more like Matthew Arnold
than something of the third century: or you come without warning on a few lines of "comparative criticism,"
as we call it—an illustration from Genesis—"God said,
Let there be Light, and there was Light" used for a
specimen of the exalted way of saying things. Generally, you have a sense that this author's lineage is mysterious after the fashion of Melchisedek's.

Well, to our point—Longinus finds that the conditions of lofty utterance are five: of which the first is
by far the most important. And this foremost condition is innate: you either have it or you have not. Here
it is:

"Elsewhere," says Longinus, "I have written as follows:
'Sublimity is the echo of a great soul.' Hence even a bare
idea sometimes, by itself and without a spoken word will
excite admiration, just because of the greatness of soul
implied. Thus the silence of Ajax in the underworld is great
and more sublime than words."

You remember the passage, how Odysseus meets that
great spirit among the shades and would placate it,

would "make up" their quarrel on earth now, with carneying words:

"Ajax, son of noble Telamon, wilt thou not then, even in death forget thine anger against me over that cursed armour. . . . Nay, there is none other to blame but Zeus: he laid thy doom on thee. Nay, come hither, O my lord, and hear me and master thine indignation."
So I spake, but he answered me not a word, but strode from me into the Darkness, following the others of the dead that be departed.

Longinus goes on:

It is by all means necessary to point this out—that the truly eloquent must be free from base and ignoble (or ill-bred) thoughts. For it is not possible that men who live their lives with mean and servile aims and ideas should produce what is admirable and worthy of immortality. Great accents we expect to fall from the lips of those whose thoughts are dignified.

Believe this and it surely follows, as concave implies convex, that by daily converse and association with these great ones we take their breeding, their manners, earn their magnanimity, make ours their gifts of courtesy, unselfishness, mansuetude, high-seated pride, scorn of pettiness, wholesome plentiful jovial laughter.

> He that of such a height hath built his mind,
>   And rear'd the dwelling of his soul so strong
>   As neither fear nor hope can shake the frame
> Of his resolvèd powers, nor all the wind
>   Of vanity or malice pierce to wrong
>   His settled peace, or to disturb the same;

What a fair seat hath he, from whence he may
The boundless wastes and wilds of man survey!

And with how free an eye doth he look down
Upon these lower regions of turmoil!
Where all the storms of passions mainly beat
On flesh and blood; where honour, power, renown,
Are only gay afflictions, golden toil;
Where greatness stands upon as feeble feet
As frailty doth; and only great doth seem
To little minds, who do it so esteem. , . . .

Knowing the heart of man is set to be
The centre of this world, about the which
These revolutions of disturbances
Still roll; where all th' aspects of misery
Predominate; whose strong effects are such
As he must bear, being powerless to redress;
And that, unless above himself he can
Erect himself, how poor a thing is man!

IX

If the exhortation of these verses be somewhat too high and stoical for you, let me return to Longinus and read you, from his concluding chapter, a passage you may find not inapposite to these times, nor without a moral:

"It remains" [he says] "to clear up, my dear Terentianus, a question which a certain philosopher has recently mooted. I wonder," he says, "as no doubt do many others, how it happens that in our time there are men who have the gift of persuasion to the utmost extent, and are well fitted for public life, and are keen and ready, and particularly rich

¹ Samuel Daniel, *Epistle to the Lady Margaret, Countess of Cumberland.*

in all the charms of language, yet there no longer arise really lofty and transcendent natures unless it be quite peradventure. So great and world-wide a dearth of high utterance attends our age. Can it be," he continued, "we are to accept the common cant that democracy is the nursing mother of genius, and that great men of letters flourish and die with it? For freedom, they say, has the power to cherish and encourage magnanimous minds, and with disseminated eager mutual rivalry and the emulous thirst to excel. Moreover, by the prizes open under a popular government, the mental faculties of orators are perpetually practised and whetted, and as it were, rubbed bright, so that they shine free as the state itself. Whereas to-day," he went on, "we seem to have learnt as an infant-lesson that servitude is the law of life; being all wrapped, while our thoughts are yet young and tender, in observances and customs as in swaddling clothes, bound without access to that fairest and most fertile source of man's speech (I mean Freedom) so that we are turned out in no other guise than that of servile flatterers. And servitude (it has been well said) though it be even righteous, is the cage of the soul and a public prison-house."

But I answered him thus.—"It is easy, my good sir, and characteristic of human nature, to gird at the age in which one lives. Yet consider whether it may not be true that it is less the world's peace that ruins noble nature than this war iliimitable which holds our aspirations in its fist, and occupies our age with passions as with troops that utterly plunder and harry it. The love of money and the love of pleasure enslave us, or rather, as one may say, drown us body and soul in their depths. For vast and unchecked wealth marches with lust of pleasure for comrade, and when one opens the gate of house or city, the other at once enters and abides. And in time these two build nests in the hearts of men, and quickly rear a progeny only too legitimate: and the ruin within the man is gradually consummated as the sublimities of his soul wither away and fade, and in ecstatic contemplation of our mortal parts we omit to exalt, and come to neglect in nonchalance, that within us which is immortal."

I had a friend once who, being in doubt with what picture to decorate the chimney-piece in his library, cast away choice and wrote up two Greek words—$\Psi\Upsilon X H\Sigma$ $'IATPEION$; that is, the hospital—the healing-place—of the soul.

INDEX

A

Acts of the Apostles, The, 186, 187
Addison, Joseph, 164, 215
Adonais, Shelley's, 89
Adrian VI, Pope, 86
Æschylus, 1, 135, 203, 206
Æsop and Rhodopè, Landor's, 131
Agamemnon, The, 88
Aims of Literary Study, The, 7
Allegro, L', 69, 70, 71
Ameipsias, 23
Anatomy of Melancholy, Burton's, 175
Ancient Mariner, The, 66
Andersen, Hans Christian, 52
Anglo-Saxon Chronicle, The, 174
Annual Register, The, 174
Anti-Jacobin, The, 218
Apologia, Newman's, 175
Arabian Nights, M. Gulland's, 48
Arabian Nights, The, 156
Arber, 111
Aristophanes, 23, 165
Aristotle, 1, 28, 54, 57, 58, 65, 67, 135, 144, 167, 169, 196, 233
Arnold, Matthew, 43, 112, 118, 139, 172, 173, 231, 240
Arraignment of Paris, Peele's, 89
As You Like It, 79
Aulnoy, Madame D', 48
Aurispa, 236
Austen, Jane, 115, 218, 222

B

Bacon, Francis, 24, 25, 26, 81, 106, 141, 174, 231
Bagehot, Walter, 40, 127
Bailey, Philip James, 175
Baker, Sir William, 192
Balder Dead, 184, 185
Ballad, The, 61
Barbour, John, 174

Bede, 234
Beethoven, 147
Beginnings of Poetry, Dr. Gummere's, 61, 62, 64, 65
Beowulf, 112
Berkeley, George, 215
Berners, 216
Bible, The, 109, 141 *et seq.*
Bible, Geneva, The, 175
Blackwood's Magazine, 89
Blair, Robert, 175
Blake, William, 37, 174
Boileau, 216
Bologna, University of, 82
Book of Nonsense, Lear's, 124
Boswell, James, 105, 174
Bottomley, Horatio, 208
Brady, Nicholas, 192
Brooke, Stopford, 106
Brown, Dr. John, 63
Browne, Sir Thomas, 164, 208, 212, 213
Browning, Elizabeth Barrett, 80
Browning, Robert, 5, 7, 17, 171, 174, 231
Bruce, The, Barbour's, 174
Bunyan, John, 109, 150, 151, 164, 172
Burke, Edmund, 106, 117, 130, 175, 215
Burns, Robert, 109, 148
Burton, Robert, 175
Butcher, Professor, 144
Byron, Lord, 5, 89, 190

C

Cabinet des Fées, Le, 48
Cambridge Essays on Education, Inge's essay in, 125
Cambridge History of English Literature, The, 5, 171, 234
Cambridge Platonists, The, 32, 217

Studies in Literature

By
Sir Arthur Quiller Couch, M. A.

Familiar discourses by the popular novelist and distinguished professor of English Literature at Cambridge—Among the subjects brilliantly discussed are "The Commerce of Thought," "Ballads," "Some Seventeenth Century Poets," "The Poetry of George Meredith," "Thomas Hardy," and "Swinburne."

G. P. Putnam's Sons

New York   London

On the Art of Writing

By

Sir Arthur Quiller-Couch

In a fresh and untrammeled manner the author deals with the craftsmanship as well as the content of letters. The scope of the volume is indicated by the appended chapter titles: "The Practice of Writing," "On the Difference between Verse and Prose," "Interlude," "On Jargon," "On the Special Difficulty of Prose," "On the Lineage of English Literature," "English Literature in our Universities."

G. P. Putnam's Sons

New York   London

The
Lure of the Pen

By

Flora Klickman

8°

An almost indispensable volume for those who aspire to write for publication, written by an editor of wide experience.

"For real solid sensible advice in the matter of writing and selling stories Miss Klickman romps in an easy winner."—ROBERT BENCHLEY in the *New York World.*

G. P. Putnam's Sons

New York   London